P9-DNK-815

On the front fly leaf: the architects'
first conception of The Lincoln
National Life Insurance Company's
home office on Harrison Street.

EASY
TO
REMEMBER

Copyright © 1980, The Lincoln
National Life Insurance Company,
1300 S. Clinton Street,
Fort Wayne, Indiana 46801.

EASY
TO
REMEMBER

A BRIEF HISTORY
OF THE
LINCOLN NATIONAL
LIFE INSURANCE
COMPANY

BY
MARK E. NEELY JR.

ACKNOWLEDGMENTS

Thomas A. Watson, then the chief executive officer of Lincoln National Life, first encouraged me to write a history of the Company for its seventy-fifth anniversary. I am grateful for the opportunity he gave me and especially for his faith that a historian with no expertise in life insurance could perform the task. I have always suspected (and hoped) that he saw my lack of knowledge of the industry as a partial liability only. I think he felt that if a layman like me could gain an understanding of the Company's history, the resulting book would be intelligible to other readers unschooled in the technicalities of life insurance. I have written this brief history with that goal in mind. He particularly enjoined me *not* to write a history that would be of interest only to the highest-ranking officers of this corporation. Whatever the degree of success in this attempt, I admire his willingness to see this history as something more than a mirror in which the executives could admire their own good work.

There are no skeletons in the Lincoln closet. I have seen everything I asked to see. Ian Rolland, the current chief executive officer, told me I could read every letter in his files, including the ones on his desk at the moment I asked. This openness runs completely counter to the fevered suspicions of many writers outside the business world who feel that a corporation always hides some of its history from inquiring eyes. When I asked Rolland whether I should quote a letter by this Company's founder, Arthur F. Hall, in which he spelled out explicitly how much money the corporation made on a certain kind of business, Rolland replied: "Leave it in. It's a fact."

More people than I could name in many pages helped me with this work. Watson, Rolland, and Henry Rood granted long interviews in which they answered the nosiest of questions. Michael Marchese read every chapter to help steer me clear of errors born of my inexperience in dealing with the principles of life insurance. Marilyn Steele likewise read the whole manuscript with an eye to keeping it readable for those who are not life insurance executives. Both gave me the benefit of their very helpful criticisms and offered constant encouragement in the bargain. Ian Rolland took time from his crowded schedule to give the manuscript a careful reading and offered numerous helpful suggestions and criticisms. Henry Rood took great interest in the project and helped the manuscript in many ways. Unfortunately, my ability to meet these criticisms too often fell short of the readers' abilities to discern faults, and full responsibility for whatever errors of fact or interpretation remain in this book is mine.

My Assistant, Mary Jane Hubler, helped both by reading and criticizing the manuscript and by absorbing some of the burden of office work I had to shirk to complete this history. I owe her a big debt. Jewel Fowler, my secretary, typed the manuscript, often from a virtually indecipherable scrawl, without complaint and with conscientious accuracy. My wife not only endured uncomplainingly while I neglected home for the office and this manuscript but also spent a weekend she could ill-afford away from her own work on Lafayette to read and criticize—sharply—the final manuscript. Gene Zastrow of Zastrow Studios, Inc., treated the book's design not as a job but as an opportunity and dressed the text up in his finest style.

I owe a special debt to Clyde Cover, who took a deep interest in the history of the Lincoln. The materials he gathered, and the probing analysis he made of many interesting problems in the Company's history had a great influence on this manuscript. Without his ground-breaking work, this brief history would have been impossible to produce.

The general encouragement and genuine curiosity shown by everyone in the Company who was conscious that I was at work on this book constantly sustained me. These factors always made the task seem worthwhile. What helped the most, however, was the inherent fascination I found in the letters, memoranda, and reminiscences of the people who made the seventy-five years of Lincoln National Life's history easy to remember.

Mark E. Neely, Jr.

Mark E. Neely, Jr.
Fort Wayne, Indiana
January 28, 1980

CONTENTS

An Undistinguished Ancestry

His parents came "of undistinguished families," Abraham Lincoln said in a typically brief autobiographical statement in 1859. The ancestry of the Lincoln National Life Insurance Company was much the same. Its parent, in some sense, was the Fraternal Assurance Society of America, a member of the undistinguished but large family of fraternal insurance companies which flourished around the turn of the century. Lincoln National Life's origins were undeniably humble, but like Abraham Lincoln himself, it grew to greatness.

Around the turn of the century, Americans took an increased interest in their ethnic identities. Anglo-Saxons swelled their chests and thrilled to Theodore Roosevelt's shrill proclamations of racial pride. Americans of more recent immigrant stock likewise banded together for mutual help and pride. Fraternal insurance companies were in part an outgrowth of this first era of seeking a firm group identity in an ever-growing, complex, and varied American society. Many of these societies appealed to common religious, racial, or vocational interest; almost all exuded the rhetoric if not the spirit of the fraternal lodge. From the United Brethren Mutual Aid Society of Lebanon, Pennsylvania, to the Northwestern Masonic Aid of Chicago and the Chosen Order of Friends of Indianapolis, these associations invoked various honorific titles and rituals but worked on the same—unsound—principles.

The fraternal idea was to bring together a group who would purchase insurance by assessment. As policyholders died, members of the fraternal would be assessed higher premiums in order to pay the claims. The idea of assessment was to "pass the hat when claims arise" or to "keep your reserve in your pocket." Fraternals could provide cheaper insurance than fixed-premium, legal reserve insurance companies, which collected premiums three times greater than the benefits paid in any year. Fraternals were the principal source of insurance for low- and middle-income families, the life insurance sold by the large legal reserve companies being mostly the province of the well-to-do. Fraternals, in addition to appealing to ethnic or local pride and to offering insurance at "cost" or with a "natural premium," also appealed to persons who were prejudiced against big business.

The problem of all fraternals was that they defied the laws of nature. As the members of the original group got older, more and more of them died. Assessments soon rose to so high a level that the remaining members were unwilling or unable to pay them. It was difficult to recruit new young members and impossible to attract them once the premiums began to rise. Eventually, most such companies ended in receivership.

There was another problem with fraternals: it was difficult to tell those organized out of a genuine desire for mutual self-help from those that were organized to enrich the managers at the expense of the policyholders. The latter were purely commercial projects disguised as fraternal enterprises by a ritual mumbo-jumbo. The Fraternal Assurance Society of America was almost certainly among the latter kind.

The Fraternal Assurance Society of America, founded in Fort Wayne, Indiana, in 1902, was one of at least nine companies organized by Wilbur Wynant around the turn of the century. Wynant was a man in a hurry.

An Undistinguished Ancestry

Martin Kemp (top) and Perry Randall (bottom), a somewhat unlikely pair, were united by their work for the Fraternal Assurance Society of America. Caricatures are from Bert J. Griswold's Some Fort Wayne Phizes (Fort Wayne: Archer Printing Co., 1904).

Born in a log cabin in Jasper County in 1870, he attended school in Larwill for perhaps eight years. For a time he taught school—the traditional nineteenth-century occupation of young men waiting for something better to come along. He worked as a brakeman on the Pennsylvania Railroad. He learned about the insurance business and began organizing fraternal companies. He came to Fort Wayne as a perfect stranger to set up the Fraternal in 1902. His previous insurance company credits included the Protected Home Circle (Pennsylvania) and the Supreme Tribe of Ben Hur (Indiana).

As fraternals were not required by law to maintain a reserve against future claims, they were easy to organize. The initial capital came from the sale of policies or from loans. There was supposed to be no profit, of course. The manager was to run the society strictly for the benefit of its members, using the premiums only for "reasonable" expenses. The whole thing was cemented with the spirit of the fraternal lodge. The company's officers had *opera bouffe* titles like "Supreme Past President." The only really important officer besides Wynant was the "Supreme Sergeant at Arms," a man named Martin Kemp. He was a foreman in the Pennsylvania Railroad Yard and had been active in fraternal lodge work. Doubtless, he was present for his expertise in fraternal ritual.

Wynant's promotional abilities were prodigious, and, though new in town, he managed to attract to his scheme a group of supporters drawn from the more substantial and civic-minded citizens of Fort Wayne. Perry Randall, the Supreme President, was the oldest and most eminent of the founders. He was born in Avilla, Indiana, in 1847. He attended public schools in Fort Wayne, where he graduated from high school in 1867. He went to the University of Michigan, earning a baccalaureate degree in 1871 and a law degree in 1873. He returned to live the rest of his life in Fort Wayne. He established a law practice, became president of the Smith and Randall Lumber Company and a director of the Tri-State Building and Loan Association, and was active in many programs for civic betterment. He was a Mason and a director of the Commercial Club. Not all of Randall's ventures were successful. He invested in a furniture company, a china store, a hat company, a shoe store, a livery stable, a sawmill, and a bank—all enterprises that failed. His investment in the Fraternal Assurance Society of America would not change his luck.

Other founders were prominent businessmen. Frank K. Safford, 46, was a food wholesaler. Fremont L. Jones, 47, was the founder of the Troy Laundry. Ernest W. Cook, 41, was secretary of both the Allen County Loan and Savings Association and the Citizens Trust Company. Howell C. Rockhill, 46, was one of the publishers of the Fort Wayne *Journal-Gazette*. Fay Randall, 24, was Perry Randall's son; he ran a real estate and loan office and was president of the Randall Wheel Company and the Randall Motor Car Company.

Professional men associated with the Fraternal were Dr. Calvin H. English, 45, the Medical Director; the Reverend J. Webster Bailey, minister of the Plymouth Congregational Church; and lawyer Daniel B. Ninde, 34, the Supreme Councillor. The Supreme Past President, a figurehead who lent his name to the stationery, was Newton W. Gilbert, onetime Lieutenant Governor of Indiana and soon to be a member of the United States House of Representatives.

It was an odd association: Fort Wayne's commercial elite, the leader of a rather exclusive religious minority who clung to an old New England religion in an overwhelmingly German town, a doctor, and a lawyer in league with a young and unknown promoter. There was more than mere corn in Wynant's promotional efforts: the Fraternal had a Supreme "Past" President the day it was organized. Without doubt, this was one of those fraternals organized primarily for gain. Apparently it was common for a town's elite to join such an enterprise, even when they knew little of the principles of life insurance. The *Western Underwriter* complained in the very year the Fraternal was founded that "these men who give their names know nothing about life insurance, but it tickles their vanity to have their names paraded before the public as officers of an institution. . . . Life insurance is too serious a matter to trifle with and men of influence should see the wrong they are perpetrating upon their fellows in sanctioning a flimsy scheme of becoming directors or officers."

It did not take the Fort Wayne men long to see the error of their ways. Wynant's pattern of operation was to found a company, reap considerable benefits in the early period of operation when premiums were plentiful and before many benefits had to be paid the policyholders, and move on to greener pastures. Those pastures in 1904, when Wynant resigned as Supreme Manager, were the fields of Indiana's oil boom (hence Wynant's perch atop a derrick in this 1904 caricature by local historian and political cartoonist, Bert J. Griswold). The Fraternal sold two thousand policies in its first two years. Only 528 policies were sold in 1904. The members of the board were assessed on several occasions to cover expenses. As early as January, 1903, a six hundred dollar assessment established a $4,200 bank deposit to pay 1904 death claims "should . . . funds prove inadequate for such purposes." In 1905 only ninety-two policies were sold.

The board members sought a new manager for the financially ailing Fraternal in 1905. After Wynant's departure, management fell to the reluctant Mr. Ninde, just elected County Prosecutor and in no position to reorganize and revitalize a failing business. Prospects were bleak. Who, after all, would want the job?

The attractiveness of a job offer is a function both of the nature of the job itself (in this case, difficult to say the least) and of the circumstances of the job-seeker. Far-away events, having to do with politics and journalism as well as business, would make the right man available. His name was Arthur F. Hall.

Wilbur Wynant. Caricature from Some Fort Wayne Phizes.

Years of Peril

William B. Paul. Caricature from Some Fort Wayne Phizes.

1905 was a landmark year in the history of the American life insurance industry. In September of that year the New York Legislative Insurance Investigation Committee, commonly called the Armstrong Committee (after its chairman, State Senator William W. Armstrong), began to take testimony from life insurance executives on questionable practices in the industry. The evidence of corporate contributions to political parties and legislators, speculative investments, nepotism, and other practices in the realm of high finance created a sensation, the more so because it was the first big "scandal" in the industry since 1877.

The Lincoln National Life Insurance Company was already founded by the time the Armstrong Committee met, and it is incorrect to link its founding directly to the circumstances created by that famous investigation. However, the events leading up to the Armstrong investigation had a great deal of effect on the beginnings of Lincoln National Life. The setting of the Lincoln's birth was the Progressive Era. Theodore Roosevelt was President of the United States, and muckraking—Roosevelt himself coined the word by recalling a character in *The Pilgrim's Progress*—was the rage in journalism. The year Wilbur Wynant left the Fraternal, Thomas W. Lawson began publishing "Frenzied Finance: The Story of the Amalgamated," serialized in a popular magazine called *Everybody's.* Lawson was a financier who reportedly made fifty million dollars in financial dealings involving the Standard Oil Company and Amalgamated Copper. After exposing the "system" of watered stocks and wild borrowing in the Amalgamated promotion, Lawson exposed "the life insurance combine" in the December, 1904 issue of *Everybody's.* The largest life insurance companies, he said, were "the most potent factor in the 'system.'"

When an internal struggle for control of the Equitable Life Assurance Society erupted into the public press in February of 1905, the story had dramatic impact in a world made sensitive to the importance of the life insurance industry in finance. It would lead directly to the Armstrong investigation that fall. Whatever the effect on Equitable's policyholders and management, the scandal scared the company's agents to death.

Arthur Fletcher Hall was a new Equitable agent in Indianapolis. No sooner had he become an agent, however, than he noted that "business here in the city has become extraordinarily hard to write"; he was "seriously handicapped on account of conditions in New York." He had lost two $100,000 policies on W. C. Bobbs and C. W. Merrill of the Bobbs-Merrill Company, famous book publishers, and another $50,000 case as well. Hall was confident that he could "get good men in ordinary times and . . . write a good personal business in ordinary times, but the present conditions make the accomplishment of either impossible."

William B. Paul, 27, was having even worse trouble. As Equitable's District Manager in Fort Wayne, he was an experienced life-insurance man, once a Prudential employee and for three years or more an Equitable man. Equitable's troubles in New York led them to close their Fort Wayne office, and Mr. Paul was unemployed.

Capable men were available, but was the economic and political climate right for establishing a life insurance company? The threatening atmosphere of scandal and possible government regulation, it seems, should have scared away investors, especially those who had already been burned by Wynant's fraternal scheme. But the New York investigation and the literature of exposure which led up to it had different effects on different people in different parts of the United States. Businessmen who read the literature closely noted how profitable life insurance stocks had been in the past. Midwesterners sensed opportunity in the Easterners' loss: with the giant Eastern companies temporarily discredited and preoccupied with investigations and internal problems, the field looked wide open for small new companies in other regions of the country.

As the Fraternal's directors sought a manager for the Company, they somehow learned of Mr. Paul's availability. He must have been the link to fellow-Equitable employee Hall, otherwise unknown in Fort Wayne. Several factors could have influenced the decision to restructure the Fraternal as a legal reserve company, but the fact that Hall and Paul were veterans of legal reserve companies was important. The Indiana insurance laws, as amended in 1903, also gave legal sanction to the formation of legal reserve companies on the full preliminary term valuation basis rather than the full net level premium basis. The former method of computing the level of reserves a company must establish in the early period of the policy permitted a company to devote a substantial part of the first-year premium to expenses (the computation on the full net level premium basis always resulted in a reserve figure that absorbed most of the first-year premium). For a new company, forced to compete with the premium levels offered by the established companies with large reserves, the old full net premium method posed a nearly unbearable strain. Indiana's law helped ease that strain. Moreover, the Fraternal's investors had reason to be suspicious of the soundness of the fraternal or assessment principle and to want to turn to something different.

By May 15, 1905 a preliminary agreement had been drawn up. The capital stock would be $200,000 (two thousand $100-shares), but the company could start in business when $100,000 was raised. Thirty-three Fort Wayne citizens signed the articles of incorporation on May 29th; thirty-nine had signed the preliminary agreement and subscribed to buy stock (see Appendix).

When he was weighing the offer to come to Fort Wayne in May, Hall aptly described the group as "the richest and most prominent men in that town." This was an auspicious beginning. For, though these investors probably knew no more about life insurance than the Fraternal's original investors (indeed, some of the most important investors had been involved with the Fraternal), they were now in league not with the adventurer Wynant but with legal reserve life insurance men.

Years of Peril

The name of the Company would be The Lincoln National Life Insurance Company. Perry Randall suggested the name, probably as a symbol of integrity in an industry temporarily identified with corruption. It struck a sympathetic note with Hall, whose mother cherished a dried rose distributed to her when Lincoln's remains were on view in Indianapolis in 1865. The enterprising Hall wrote Lincoln's son Robert to ask him for a photograph of his father to appear on the Company's letterhead. Robert answered on August 3, 1905:

PULLMAN BUILDING,
CHICAGO.

Manchester, Vermont,
August third, 1905.

Arthur F. Hall, Esq.,
    Secretary, The Lincoln National Life
        Insurance Company,
            Fort Wayne, Indiana.

Dear Sir:

        Replying to your note of July
28th, I find no objection whatever to the use
of a portrait of my father upon the letterhead of such a life insurance company named
after him as you describe; and I take pleasure
in enclosing you, for that purpose, what I regard as a very good photograph of him.

        Very truly yours,

        Robert T. Lincoln

Robert Todd Lincoln.

*Robert Todd Lincoln sent the famous
"five-dollar-bill" photograph of his father.*

Replying to your note of July 28th, I find no objection whatever to the use of a portrait of my father upon the letterhead of such a life insurance company named after him as you describe; and I take pleasure in enclosing you, for that purpose, what I regard as a very good photograph of him.

"Choosing a name," as Hall said in later years, "didn't establish a life insurance company." Hall did that, and the first thirty-seven years of the history of the Lincoln are inextricably interwoven with his life. Born on May 11, 1872 in Baxter Springs, Kansas, Hall was the youngest child of a Union army veteran and wholesale milliner from Indiana, Truman Hall, who died before Arthur was one year old. Harriet (Beeler) Hall, now a widow, decided to return to Indianapolis with her children, George, Emma, and Arthur. The family's circumstances were precarious, and Arthur became a newsboy for the Indianapolis *News* at age fourteen. In 1889 he quit high school before graduation to become a printer's devil for the competing Indianapolis *Journal*. A printer's devil was little more than an errand boy, but for Arthur Hall it was all the *entree* he needed. In 1900 he became Advertising Manager and in 1902 Assistant Business Manager. In 1904 the *Journal* was sold, and Hall was looking for a job. In about a year's time he managed Indiana circulation for the *Chicago Tribune*, promoted a new magazine for the Bobbs-Merrill Publishing Company, and was an agent for The Equitable.

Arthur Fletcher Hall (left) at age eighteen with his brother. Photograph from Wilson's Sunbeam Gallery in Indianapolis.

Years of Peril

Hall had been an Equitable agent only about four months when he got wind of the Fort Wayne Company's formation. He had already subscribed $5,000 to the Lincoln when he wrote Equitable's General Manager in Indianapolis, explaining:

Arthur F. Hall.

Samuel M. Foster. Caricature from Some Fort Wayne Phizes.

During the last thirty days I have had offers from different companies, and several very attractive ones, but have turned them down without consideration until this past week. There is now a new company in process of organization in Fort Wayne, Indiana. It is being organized by prominent men, among them, Presidents of seven banks and trust companies. These gentlemen have offered me one of the Vice Presidencies of the Company with the idea that I should have some Agency organization duties. It is proposed to give me a very liberal first year's commission and renewal on all business going on the books of the company. Necessarily I seriously consider accepting the proposition. While I have such a thing in mind I deem it appropriate that I say to you that I will place my resignation in your hands if you so desire it, although I have not decided at all to accept the proposition. I truly believe that if the Equitable trouble were settled today I would not consider any proposition except to stay with the Equitable in the work I had begun with it. . . .

I should like to know whether or not you have any assurances from the East of an early settlement of our trouble and what the Home Office thinks of my continuing with the company. It may be that under present conditions they will welcome the opportunity to dispense with my services. May I not have some expression from you?

Equitable's troubled General Manager could make no very soothing assurances, and Hall was therefore present at the new company's organizational meeting in Fort Wayne in June.

At that meeting Paul became Vice President and Hall Secretary of the Lincoln National Life Insurance Company. An augury of Hall's exceptional talents lay in the board's choice, within a month's time, of Hall as manager of the new company. He thus very quickly eclipsed Mr. Paul, who soon lost his job and remembered the loss of this brief opportunity for fame and fortune with increasing bitterness as the Lincoln grew in size and stature over the years.

The President was Samuel Monell Foster. Like all the other officers except the Secretary, he served without salary. He was only the titular head of the Company, far too busy with his factory which manufactured ladies' clothing and with the recently organized (March, 1905) German American Bank to run a life insurance company. Still, he added essential prestige and financial acumen. Foster was born on a farm in New York. He quit school at thirteen to work in the dry goods business. He and his brother worked in the same trade in Troy, New York. After three years, Foster quit and returned to the family farm to work in the day and educate himself at night. At age twenty-four, he went to Yale, graduated in three years, and was elected to Phi Beta Kappa. After a brief career in the newspaper business in Ohio, he joined another brother in Fort Wayne and began to manufacture women's shirtwaist dresses. He was so successful that he could found a bank in 1905. He provided the introductions to the right people that the stranger from Indianapolis needed.

Hall moved to Fort Wayne in September. His annual salary was not large. The contract guaranteed only $2,600, but the Board offered a good deal more than that as long as the Company was doing well. Hall received a commission on all renewal premiums on life insurance paid to the Company each year. Thus the canny Directors tied Hall's compensation directly to the success of the infant company. Production schedules through January 1, 1921 provided minimum levels of business necessary for the compensation arrangement to take effect—from one million dollars by 1907 to fifty-three million by 1921. Basing the Secretary's salary on premium income was illegal in some states, although not in Indiana, and Hall's arrangement drew criticism from Best's Insurance Reports. The arrangement proved satisfactory, however, and criticism of it gradually dissipated.

The Lincoln National Life Insurance Company opened for business in September of 1905 with one stenographer and three agents. The tiny office was in the White National Bank building. Employing his bookkeeping experience from his Indianapolis newspaper days, Hall devised the system of accounts and opened the books himself. The agents were William Bishop, Max Blitz, and the chief executive officer, Arthur Hall.

The earliest photograph of Hall in the Lincoln National Life office, probably taken in 1908.

The Company's first policy.

The Lincoln National Life Insurance Company

OF FORT WAYNE, INDIANA

No P. 1. $ 500 00

AGE 37 PREMIUM $ 11 25

For value received, hereby promises to pay Five hundred Dollars in the manner and subject to the conditions and agreements set forth herein, which are understood to be a part of this contract as fully as if recited over the signatures hereto affixed

Dated at Fort Wayne, Ind. The First Day of September Nineteen Hundred and five

The Lincoln National Life Insurance Co. By David M. Foster President, and Arthur F. Hall Secretary.

The Amount of this Policy, as stated above, will be paid, upon receipt at the Home Office of the Company in the city of Fort Wayne, Indiana, of satisfactory proofs of the death of Emma A. Bishop the insured hereunder, of Fort Wayne State of Indiana to Wm C. Bishop or, in event of his prior decease, to the insured's executors, administrators, or assigns, deducting therefrom any indebtedness then existing against the policy.

This insurance is granted in consideration of the written and printed application for this policy, which is hereby made a part of this contract, and of the payment in advance of Eleven 75/100 **Dollars** and of the payment of a like sum on or before the First day of September in every year thereafter, during the continuance of this contract.

This insurance is based upon the American Experience Table of Mortality and three and one-half per cent. interest, and for the first year is term insurance, and in consideration of the premium therefor, as above required, this insurance is continued as a whole life policy by the payment of further premiums thereafter as herein provided.

This policy shall not take effect until the first premium shall have been actually paid while the insured is in good health, and is issued and accepted by the parties in interest subject to the Provisions, Privileges and Options on pages two and three, which are referred to and made a part of this contract.

ORDINARY LIFE—CONTINUOUS PREMIUMS—NON-PARTICIPATING

Though Bishop had sold insurance for the old Fraternal, the results of rewriting the Fraternal's policies as Lincoln policies were disappointing. E. E. Perry, apparently a temporarily idle lawyer in Perry Randall's law firm, helped Bishop rewrite the policies. $560,000 of outstanding Fraternal insurance produced only $105,000 of insurance for the new company. The founders of the Lincoln had hoped for $300,000.

Selling legal reserve life insurance was a different proposition from selling fraternal insurance—and selling life insurance in 1905 was a different proposition from what it is today. William C. Bishop, a former house painter, had worked for the Fraternal, moving from Fort Wayne to Bluffton to establish the Fraternal's business in that rural area. A member of Plymouth Congregational Church (like the Fraternal's Supreme Chaplain) and of the Moose Lodge, Knights of Pythias, Buffaloes, and Oddfellows Lodge, Bishop was doubtless adept at the lodge work necessary in fraternal sales. But Mrs. Bishop was none too keen on living in Bluffton and was happy to move back to Fort Wayne. About five feet six inches tall and extremely obese, Bishop was likeable and energetic. He tried to make insurance more attractive by offering a premium to the buyer. He bought a truckload of statues, "Every type of a statue you could think of," his son recalled years later, "busts of Lincoln and all kinds of statues of dogs and cats," and for a time offered a statue with every policy he sold. He gave his children little whistles, hundreds of them, with the name of The Lincoln National Life Insurance Company on them to give to their schoolmates. He pressed his daughter's suitors to buy life insurance, and, as his son recalled, the unsuspecting boy "would end up either buying some insurance or he didn't come back." In 1909, 1910, and 1913 Bishop was the company's leading agent. A trip to the Mayo Clinic, however, brought Bishop a sentence of death and a tube in his stomach through which broth could pass to sustain life for a brief period; his esophagus was impassable. He came home and returned to sales work until bedridden with a fatal cancer.

Such enterprise showed in the Company's first year-end statement. $532,000 of insurance was in force. $20,859 in premiums had been paid. The company had already outgrown its little office furnished only with two straight-back chairs and an old cherry table. Early in 1906 it leased the second floor of the Independent Order of Odd Fellows Building on the northeast corner of Wayne and Calhoun Streets. The office staff, now eight people, could not fill the rooms, and the company leased three rooms to the Mercantile Accident Association. Things were going reasonably well, but thus far the Lincoln had not encountered the great bugbear of life insurance, death claims.

Sales in 1906 did not live up to Hall's expectations. He blamed the unfavorable climate for life insurance sales on Indiana's version of the Armstrong investigations, an investigation of the Indiana industry instigated by Republican Governor James Frank Hanley. 1907 was the worst year in the Company's history. In the spring the legislature considered the recommendations of Hanley's investigative committee. Among these was a proposal to outlaw full preliminary term valuation.

The Company's first offices were located in this building.

William C. Bishop.

Statement of Business to December 31, 1905.

First Policy Issued September 23, 1905.

ASSETS.		LIABILITIES.	
First mortgage loans at 6 per cent on real estate worth more than double amount loaned	$44,000.00	Net cash value of all outstanding policies, valuation made by actuary of Auditor of State, according to law	$ 2,514.00
Loans secured by stock	54,325.00		
Cash on deposit in Banks and Trust Companies	15,874.26	Premiums paid in advance	42.67
Interest accrued to Dec. 31, 1905, (not yet due)	764.05	Commissions due agents	213.41
Net deferred and unreported premiums	1,133.99	Surplus to policy holders	113,327.22
Total admitted assets	$116,097.30	Total liabilities	$116,097.30

AMOUNT OF INSURANCE IN FORCE DECEMBER 31, 1905, - $532,000.00

The Lincoln National Life Insurance Company
of Fort Wayne, Indiana

WAS organized in the fall of 1905, with an authorized capital of $200,000, and as a legal reserve company operating under the Indiana Compulsory Deposit Law for Legal Reserve Companies, which law affords the insured a greater degree of safety than is furnished by the laws of any other state in the Union.

On the 23rd day of September the Company issued its first policy and the statement given above is the record of the Company's business for the first one hundred days of its activity.

There is nothing phenomenal, nothing miraculous about the results shown in this statement. It is simply a record of what we set out to do and firmly believed that we would accomplish. **It shows a good, sound, healthy beginning** all along the line.

During the short period of fourteen weeks the **LINCOLN NATIONAL LIFE** has become firmly established in the State of Indiana, to which state it confines its business operations at the present time.

In less than four months' time it has won the unreserved confidence of the insuring public and received its endorsement to the amount of more than $700,000 insurance applied for, of which amount $532,000, with a total of $20,859, in annual premiums, has been accepted and issued to December 31, 1905.

During this same brief period, and notwithstanding the unavoidable heavy initial expenses of organizing and "getting started," the management has successfully carried out its policy of absolute conservatism and economy. Not ONE DOLLAR of the paid in capital has been needed to carry on the work. Moreover a fair margin of that part of first years' premiums by law allowed for expenses of securing business, has been saved, and as a result even the first statement shows an actual surplus of more than $3,000, exclusive of capital stock.

Nothing could be more gratifying than this proof of wise management which is destined to become the source of large dividend-returns to all policyholders under the provisions of the "ideal" policy sold by the **LINCOLN NATIONAL LIFE.**

The policy contracts of the **LINCOLN NATIONAL LIFE INSURANCE CO.** are the most **flexible** and **equitable** contracts of insurance issued, that are consistent with sound insurance principles. Aside from all guaranteed loan values, cash surrender values, paid-up values and automatic extended insurance provisions as contained in the contracts of most other companies, **the contract of the LINCOLN NATIONAL LIFE provides for an annual accounting of all dividend earnings** and makes dividends, allowed to accumulate for further profits, absolutely non-forfeitable.

For particulars regarding the "IDEAL POLICY" address
THE LINCOLN NATIONAL LIFE INSURANCE CO.,
FORT WAYNE, IND.

This provoked the Company's first great lobbying effort, conducted not by a paid lobbyist but by Hall and President Foster themselves. Foster argued that the prohibition of full preliminary term valuation would drive the infant company from the state.

The legislature failed to enact any new measures, but it nevertheless scared off many a life insurance prospect. Despite an unusually good "mortality experience" (the Company had yet to experience a death claim), the Company's capital was impaired by high sales costs. Late in the year, the board approved an assessment of stockholders to shore up the surplus, a move Hall thought necessary to counteract accusations from competing companies that the Lincoln was about to go under. The assessment was successful, and the Company reported a surplus at the end of the year, escaping the wrath of Mr. Best's report. Best, in fact, merely commented that the Company was "operating along legitimate lines" and was "solvent." Conservative underwriting by the Company's Medical Director, Dr. Calvin English, helped. When a horse kicked young Delbert Noel of Corunna, Indiana, and broke his neck in November of 1907, the Company paid its first death claim. He had paid for his new policy only three weeks before. Despite this, savings from the anticipated mortality rate continued.

New business is a mixed blessing to a life insurance company, particularly to a young one. Hall stated the problem succinctly at a 1909 stockholders' meeting:

The Company's first claim check.

The loss on agents is alike in all but the old established insurance companies. We are no exception to the rule. We find it necessary to advance money to our men to go out in the field and solicit business. This money is charged to their account against their commission and renewals. When an agent quits we simply cross his balance off the books and the renewals for future years go into the general fund. Large Companies do not find it necessary to advance their agents as they employ General Agents who advance the money to subagents and the loss, if any, comes to the General Agents.

The first annual agency convention of the Lincoln National Life Insurance Company at Put-In-Bay Island, Ohio, August, 1909. Bishop is seated on the ground, Hall at the right, and Shepard at the far left. Theodore F. Ruhland is seated at Hall's right. Above Shepard, in order, are: Ninde, unidentified, unidentified, J. C. W. Coppess, W. H. Ingham, W. W. Pipes, L. R. Whyte, George B. Hall, unidentified, J. I. Brown, unidentified, and W. W. Robinson.

To control the high cost of new business Hall established an Agency Committee in 1910. Every Saturday morning at ten o'clock, Hall, Theodore F. Ruhland, Walter T. Shepard, Edwin H. Redding, and Dr. English met to consider "any agency plan or endeavor or any agency arrangement that required the outlay of money." Agents "receiving salaries, advances and other help in the shape of payment for office rents, stenographers, etc. were entirely cut out and business accepted only on a commission basis. This meant almost an entire reorganization of the agency force," Hall reported to stockholders in 1911. Ruhland resigned, and Shepard became Superintendent of Agencies at a $2,700 yearly salary.

1911 showed the solid results of the Company's austerity. The surplus nearly doubled, and Best reported that the cost of new business was "reasonably moderate, much improvement being shown." The Company began to enjoy some of the luxuries of size and wealth. Hall hired a full-time Actuary at a salary of $4,000 a year (he got the money by convincing the directors it would be better to hire a capable man than purchase the substantial amount of insurance they wished to put on Hall's valuable life). He relieved Ninde of all office duties so that he could devote his attention entirely to legal work—the beginnings of a legal department. Foster and Hall no longer had to sign all policies; Allen Lawrie became Recorder empowered to sign policies. The Company had 106 agents who were restrained from issuing more than $2,400,000 in new business in order not to strain the surplus.

The new Actuary was to prove a very important person at the Lincoln. His name was Franklin B. Mead, and he came to the Company full of facts and figures—and new ideas.

The seventh floor of the Shoaff Building was the Company's home from 1909 to 1912.

Arthur F. Hall's office around 1918.

Franklin B. Mead.

Years of Daring

Arthur Hall did not believe in one-man companies, though there was much in his life to prejudice him in their favor. He knew the importance of hiring, training, and giving rein to strong-willed and strong-minded subordinates.

One of the strongest-willed and strongest-minded was Franklin Bush Mead. Born in a middle-class home in Greenfield, Ohio, in 1875, Mead attended public schools in Cincinnati. In 1895 he entered the University of Cincinnati for two years of college education; his performance was anything but spectacular. He worked for a time for the Security Trust and Life Insurance Company of Philadelphia, a company which specialized in substandard risks, that is, in selling policies to people with health impairments or in dangerous occupations. In 1904 he returned to college, this time at the University of Michigan, from which he graduated in 1906. He continued to pursue a career in life insurance, going to work in 1908 for a year-old company in Detroit called Michigan State Life. He began to present papers at industry-wide meetings, most notably at the American Life Convention. He probably met Arthur F. Hall at one of these trade association meetings. Hall hired him in 1911.

Hall got more than a full-time actuary. Mead was an innovative and daring thinker in addition to being a meticuluously "scientific" believer in statistics. He was also a capable manager who worshipped efficiency. He had, in sum, great executive potential. Mead would devise the Company policies which made it famous in the industry and which accounted in large part for its spectacularly successful performance over the next fifty years.

Mead's personality was what one sometimes finds in a man of unusual intellect and originality. His social life was limited. He had, for instance, no use for golf. He pursued his principal after-hours passion, horticulture, with the same zeal and determination he employed on the job. His home, "Iriscrest," eventually contained four acres of flowers and shrubs. He wrote articles for several national gardening magazines and was a member of the Royal Horticultural Society of England. At his death his plants were given to the City of Fort Wayne and formed the basis of the gardens at Foster Park. His interests were broad and included rare books, Chinese ceramics, and etchings, all of which he collected. He was a gourmet and an amateur photographer. Like all omnivorous intellects, Mead's was sometimes uncritical and included an interest in "Dr. Kellogg's diet," a food fad based on avoidance of autointoxication from overeating, especially of meats. His abominable driving was so well known that the New York architect of the Lincoln's first office building could introduce Mead at a banquet by saying, ". . . when Fort Wayne has ducked into every available doorway and there isn't a traffic cop brave enough to stick to his post, you may know that he is attempting to drive his automobile, while engaged in a suave conversation with the occupant of the rear seat." He was not an active church-goer. His interests ran more to cultural organizations, the Indiana Historical Society, the Fort Wayne Art School, the Hoosier Art Salon, and the Indiana Federation of Arts.

Years of Daring

Dr. Calvin English.

The Lincoln felt the impact of Mead's advent very quickly. In 1912 when he became Secretary, Hall became First Vice-President and General Manager. Together they established aggressive but well-considered programs in substandard underwriting and reinsurance. These became hallmarks of The Lincoln National Life Insurance Company.

Mead's interest in substandard risks flowed naturally from his early experience with the Security Trust and Life of Philadelphia. In Fort Wayne he encountered no hostility to his desire to accept substandard risks. A young company hungry for business, the Lincoln hated to turn its agents' efforts down. Dr. English, the first Medical Director, wanted to accept more business by charging a higher premium for persons in dangerous occupations or with health impairments. Dr. English, in fact, accepted the first substandard policies before Mead joined the Company. As early as June 15, 1909, the Company issued a substandard policy (on a railroad engineer), but it was almost eight months before it issued another. The trouble was that Dr. English considered the risks a medical problem. Mead considered them a statistical problem, and he arrived just as statistics gathered industry-wide became available on a few classes of substandard risks. English and Mead saw eye-to-eye in regard to this kind of business, and Mead could supply the tables English needed to judge substandard risks.

The impact of the policy was enormous and quickly felt. In 1913 Mead reported that the Company rejected less than 4% of the total number of insurance applications received. The industry average was about 11%. In other words, each Lincoln agent found that the Company turned down slightly less than one of each twenty applicants he secured; an average life insurance company turned down one of each nine. Mead estimated that substandard risks accounted for 2-3% of the Company's business. He was a careful statistician and always took into account a multiplicity of variables. In the early years he duly noted that the success of the substandard program was also attributable to the avoidance of high-pressure agents (of whom he was never fond) and to the fact that the Lincoln sold insurance only in a limited geographical area, the Midwest, where most of the insured were from rural areas. The latter point made a virtue of necessity, perhaps, and betrayed a tendency in Mead's thought which was uncharacteristically backward-looking.

Even the relatively untutored Dr. English, a doctor of limited education born on a farm and not a specialist in life insurance, could see the advantages of substandard risks. And the availability of some industry-wide statistics showed that Mead was not a trailblazer. Nevertheless, he was quicker than most to realize the statistical soundness of substandard risks even for a new company and could say, probably accurately, after only one more year of substandard business that "The Company has developed its facilities in this direction to a point only attained by three or four other companies in the country." The real genius in his work for substandard risks lay in seeing quickly not only that abnormal cases could be classified statistically just as normal ones could but also that these statistics applied just as well—even better—to a new company in the Midwest as to the older giants. It was the sort of program

one expected to be tried by a large, well-established company; its implementation by a tiny company less than a decade old was remarkable.

Mead's interest in reinsurance, that is, in accepting part of the risk on a policy written by another company for a larger amount than that company's surplus could safely handle, was equally important, but it defies explanation. Whatever the cause, Mead had a knack for attracting reinsurance business. His visibility in the industry, a by-product of his technical papers at trade association meetings, helped. He quickly made Hall aware of its importance. When he made his report on the 1913 business to stockholders, Hall had rather disappointing sales figures, largely because of floods in Indiana and Ohio which prevented writing much business in the first quarter of the year. Sales were ten percent below Hall's predictions for 1913. Nevertheless, the First Vice-President could report a "handsome increase of insurance in force" by adding to the direct sales of insurance the reinsurance business which Mead had secured during the year. Lincoln National Life obtained reinsurance business from forty companies in 1913, which amounted to $886,000 of paid-for insurance. Reinsurance accounted for most of the increase in amount of insurance written over the previous year's amount. Hall was without doubt pleased with Mead's new program.

The reinsurance results for 1914 were even better, more than doubling the amount for 1913. Whether Mead realized it at first or not,

An early agency convention.

27

substandard underwriting and reinsurance were wonderfully complementary programs. As a pioneer in substandard risks, Lincoln National Life could help underwrite policies that were not only too large for other companies but which the other companies would otherwise have been unable to accept as normal insurance risks. In future years other companies would catch up to the Lincoln's level of ability in substandard underwriting, but by then the reinsurance business was so well established—and the Lincoln's experience in serving reinsurance clients so much greater—that there was no catching up to the Lincoln's lead in being an insurer of insurers.

Before the Lincoln National Life Insurance Company was a decade old, it had established business practices in the areas which would

Home office workers in front of the Lincoln Life building around 1920.

distinguish it within the industry and which accounted for its success *vis-a-vis* the many other young companies which started business around the turbulent period of the Armstrong insurance investigations: substandard underwriting and reinsurance. A third was added in 1914: assumption reinsurance or portfolio reinsurance, the acquisition of another insurance company and the assumption of its policies as the policies of the purchasing company.

The Michigan State Life Insurance Company was younger but larger than Lincoln National Life. Mead had worked there and was doubtless the source of information that the Michigan company could be purchased. Mead had always disliked high-pressure business. He knew that the Michigan State Life's business, though it had grown spectacularly, was sound. When a young, fast-growing company acquires a still younger, but faster-growing company, the transaction holds promise of excitement and sometimes mystery. After all, why would Michigan State Life stockholders want to sell?

MICHIGAN STATE LIFE INSURANCE COMPANY

DETROIT, MICHIGAN.

FREDERIC APPS President

HOME OFFICE—MAJESTIC BLDG

May 14, 1913

TO THE REPRESENTATIVES OF THE MICHIGAN STATE LIFE INSURANCE COMPANY:

The crisis which the Michigan State Life Insurance Company has passed through during the last 90 days we believe has now become beneficial to all concerned. It has disposed of every connection we may have had in the past that would have a tendency to cast a reflection upon us; it has been the means of placing our Company in the hands of clean-cut business fellows- men who are thoroughly conversant with insurance affairs and whose ideals of life and business experience have placed them at the head of the financial as well as the social world. It also has given us an opportunity to re-organize the Agency Department and bring it to a sound business basis, which is consistent with good management. It has also brought out in this particular the strong, zealous fellows- men who can write business in the face of all obstacles and who can take adverse criticism and capitalize it to the benefit of themselves as well as to the Company in soliciting business. It is this class of men that the future destinies of the Company will be guided by both from the Home Office and from an agency standpoint.

It is indeed gratifying to the officers of the Company to note the number of courageous men that now represent the Company. They have had to meet with all sorts of arguments that would have a tendency to dishearten them, they have been approached by representatives of other companies for the purpose of securing their services, and have listened to the unscrupulous comments which these men have not hesitated to make; and in the face of these obstacles we have been continually writing business and writing it on a basis that the Company could afford.

There has been no complaint on the part of the officials of the Company as to the present production of business. On the other hand they have felt gratified to think that in view of all our Company has passed through during the last 90 days that the business was so near the normal mark.

There was excitement aplenty in Lincoln National Life's acquisition of Michigan State Life. The most exciting character involved was Frederick L. Apps, a shadowy promoter who came to Michigan from Missouri, where he had been General Agent for the Missouri State Life Insurance Company. He came North with ideas of making big money fast. In 1905 he organized Frederick Apps & Company in Owosso, Michigan, apparently a life insurance agency. He was still an agent for Missouri State Life. In 1907 Michigan State Life was founded in Owosso. Apps was probably the moving force behind it, but his name did not appear on the articles of incorporation. Apps became Agency Director, and Frederick Apps & Company gained the exclusive general agent's contract for Michigan. In 1908 Apps gained the exclusive contract for the whole United States; it empowered him to effect an entire agency organization. Michigan State Life merely approved applications and issued policies; Apps did all the rest. In 1910 Apps became president of Michigan State Life, assigning the agency contract to a henchman, Howard C. Wade.

Hall's picture appeared on the cover of the Michigan State Life house organ as President of that company in 1913.

Meanwhile, Apps had founded another corporation in South Dakota, the General Founders Company. He acquired the common stock of Frederick Apps & Company and then sold the stock to General Founders for $70,000. With that money he began to purchase Michigan State Life stock. He acquired control of the company by 1910. In 1913 Apps sold $200,000 worth of stock which he controlled in the company to Arthur F. Hall and disappeared, along with his henchmen. He used capital from General Founders and two other shadowy companies organized in Michigan to purchase Michigan State Life and to keep the life insurance company healthy. When he sold his Michigan State Life stock, the other companies—which had funded his purchase of Michigan State Life stock—collapsed. Michigan State Life flourished on the capital that investors in his other corporations supplied—and lost. And Lincoln National Life bought a solid company, the one part of the phony Apps empire which he kept sound. The sale took place before the collapse of Apps' card castle. His willingness to sell was a function of his stock juggling.

What Lincoln National Life knew about Apps is unclear. Mead had worked for the company from 1908 to 1911, leaving not long after Apps became president. He knew that the company's business was sound; indeed, he had probably overseen its soundness just as he did that of Lincoln National Life. From Mead or from other contacts at the Michigan company, N. B. Ninde had heard that Apps was a shady character. A memo, probably written by Ninde, described him this way:

> Frederick Apps is a name assumed by Apps, and it is alleged that he formerly lived near Binghamton, N.Y. That some of his transactions there were of a questionable and perhaps criminal nature; so much so that Arthur Jones, his attorney, had to go down and settle them. After leaving Binghamton, Apps went to Mexico. Was engaged in a mining business or promoting of some kind. The next known of him was when he appeared in Iowa, selling Iowa insurance bonds. He later appeared in Kansas, selling bonds for the Missouri Life Insurance Company. . . . During all of this time Apps was a pretty hard drinker.

Lincoln National Life reinsured Michigan State Life's business, that is, assumed its policies as its own. The quality of the business was fine, and the Lincoln took a giant step forward with the shrewd purchase.

The acquisition and reinsurance of Michigan State Life was so successful that Hall was looking for other companies to acquire almost as soon as the deal was consummated. The Pioneer Life Insurance Company, founded in 1907 in Fargo, North Dakota, was another young company which had grown faster than the Lincoln (up to the date of the acquisition of Michigan State Life). By the end of 1916 it had $18,767,923.94 of business in force. Best's had only praise for this company on the plains. Why its stockholders were willing to sell is not at all clear, but it was probably due to economic conditions in North Dakota. Agriculture in the West entered a troubled period in 1910, and that trouble was reflected in the minutes of the company's board

In 1915 the Lincoln's agency convention went to Detroit and Mackinac Island, Michigan. At left, the dock in Detroit. Above, Hall with the agents' wives at the boat ticket office.

meetings. On July 13, 1910, for example, the secretary wrote, "Owing to the shortage of crops throughout the state, the Secretary advised that in the event the company wished to continue its present field forces, it would be necessary to make some provision to accept notes in settlement of first year's premiums, and in order to retain its present ratio of business in force, it would also be necessary to accept a great many notes in settlement of subsequent years' premiums." The minutes referred to "adverse crop conditions" in 1914 and to "adverse financial and crop conditions" again in 1915. The state's economy led to a peculiar marketing practice which relied on small-town bankers rather than insurance agents. These bankers sold policies to farmers, always short on cash, by lending money which became a certificate of deposit in the bank in the amount of the premium payment. The certificates earned high rates of interest, but—like the bulk of the company's investments (farm mortgages)—were ultimately tied to the success of the crop at year's end.

The Lincoln probably showed an interest in acquiring Pioneer Life as early as 1915. By organizing a syndicate to borrow money for the purchase, Hall was able to purchase the company's stock and reinsure its business. A great intangible benefit of the purchase was the Pioneer's agency force, which worked well in the Dakotas, Minnesota, and Montana. Because of the peculiar selling methods developed for the cash-poor arid plains, however, the Lincoln supervised the former Pioneer agents from a special agency in Minneapolis. The transaction also brought considerable executive talent with it, most notably, A. L. Dern.

The deal was consummated in 1917, adding the Pioneer's nineteen million dollars of business to the Lincoln's thirty-one million. By the end of 1917, the Lincoln's business had doubled to 63 million and produced what Hall called "disorganized office conditions." By January, 1918 one-third of the Company's employees were new clerks hired to take care of the increased business, and carpenters were knocking down walls to gain room to accommodate them.

Arthur Hall (second from left in the front row) and Franklin Mead (fifth from left) at a meeting with the Pioneer Life executives in 1916. Ninde is the man furthest to the right in the next row up.

The impact of World War I on Lincoln National Life is not easy to assess. The Company's growth continued apace during the period. Reinsurance increased dramatically from $900,000 of business in 1913 to two millions in 1914, 2-2/3 millions in 1915, 4-1/3 millions in 1916, and 9-2/3 millions in 1917. The fact that German companies were famous for their reinsurance business suggests that the war in Europe, which certainly curtailed their activities, may have offered the Lincoln new opportunities. However, as Mead reported at the beginning of 1918, 2-1/2 millions of the spectacular increase in business in 1917 "was taken over enbloc from The Pittsburgh Life which failed on account of the looting of the treasury in a most sensational manner by unscrupulous individuals who acquired temporary control of the company with the fraudulent assistance of a trust company in New York." The war apparently did not affect mortality as severely as anticipated because relatively few Americans, as Hall put it, "saw hard fighting." Hall himself devoted considerable effort to patriotic causes. He headed the fourth Liberty Loan drive in Allen County, meeting the county's quota for the first time. He was a member of the American Protective League for the Fort Wayne district, responsible apparently for supplying information on the area's loyalty and patriotic work. He was the treasurer of the Allen County Defense League, a somewhat mysterious loyalty organization.

The Company was looking inward in 1918 because of the internal problems caused by the large influx of business and the consequent large influx of untrained clerks to handle it. The principal sign of patriotic effort was the Company's purchases of Liberty Bonds. Mead, who was a financial conservative, winced at the lower rate of interest than the 6 - 6-1/2% the Lincoln customarily earned on its principal investments, farm mortgages. It especially galled him because the government used the bond money to support a credit program for American farmers. The availability of government money, of course, lowered the interest rates on farm mortgages. The year before, Mead had railed against the government's farm policies:

This is intrinsically an agricultural country where the most favorable agricultural conditions of the world prevail and it is, therefore, hard to understand why farming should be subsidized and why the farmers over the country should be able to secure their money at a less rate of interest than the merchant or any other borrower for short time paper. We believe that the farmer should pay the market rate for money and if he cannot afford to pay the market rate, the price of the commodities he produces should be increased. I believe there is no one here who will deny that he is receiving a proper price for his commodities and, therefore, the logical conclusion is that there is no reason why the government should subsidize the Land Bank so that it might get cheaper money than those engaged in other industries. The rate of interest follows the natural law and, if an attempt is made to controvert those laws by legislation, disastrous, or at least unsatisfactory, consequences will follow, just as occurs when we try to controvert any other natural law.

More dramatic in its impact on life insurance than the war was the influenza epidemic that hit the United States in October. It struck only in the last quarter of the year, yet 60% of the Company's 1918 mortality

The beginning of a Company outing around 1920.

The Elektron Building was the Company's home from 1912 to 1923.

was due to flu claims. 1918 death claims almost totalled the amount of all previous death claims in the Company. The Company covered up a $250,000 decrease in capital and surplus with a $300,000 loan from the members of the Executive Committee. Once again, however, Hall was optimistic, and once again his optimism was justified. He saw that the government's issuing war risk insurance on men in the armed forces and the ability of the industry to pay influenza claims were a boon to the industry: "The results of the approval given to life insurance by our government and the results of the wonderful service performed by life insurance in paying influenza claims, have I believe, advanced the cause of life insurance as twenty years of ordinary time would not have done." Sales jumped in December and January, and in 1919 Mead told dividend-less stockholders that the $250,000 loss on the flu epidemic "will represent in the long run a profitable investment for the Company, as the outlook is that the claims due to the epidemic and the war have popularized insurance to such an extent that the Company will secure a more profitable return for the expenditure of the $250,000, than might have been secured by an expenditure of a like amount over a period of time toward the natural expansion of business." Mead was not whistling in the dark. The years of peril were over, and the Lincoln National Life was soon to reap the rewards of daring.

A summer day about 1920 brings Lincoln Life workers out on the sidewalk.

This 1919 advertisement echoed President Woodrow Wilson's "Fourteen Points," his proposed peace terms after the First World War.

September 18, 1919   THE INSURANCE SALESMAN   19

More than 4 millions a month

Story of the Amazing Success of

THE LINCOLN LIFE

told in Fourteen Points

FIRST:—ALL LINCOLN LIFE agency contracts are made direct with the Company.

SECOND:—Agency contracts cannot be canceled by the Company, without cause, on thirty days' notice.

THIRD:—The Company is clean through and through.

FOURTH:—It is not a One-Man Company. Even the entire Board of Directors controls only 42 percent of its stock.

FIFTH:—Service to policyholders and agents is a keynote. In normal times 60 percent of new policies are in the mails the very day the applications arrive.

SIXTH:—The Company issues both participating and non-participating insurance.

SEVENTH:—The Company insures women at the same premiums as men.

EIGHTH:—The Company insures all sorts of hazardous risks, such as miners, railroad men and electricians.

NINTH:—The Company issues Double Accident insurance with Dismemberment benefits.

TENTH:—The Company issues a Disability Clause which pays 1 percent of the face of the policy per month, no deductions being made from the sum payable at maturity of the policy.

ELEVENTH:—The Company issues an Exchangeable policy to children as young as one year.

TWELFTH:—Policies are issued on 92 percent of its applications. Of the remainder 4 percent are modified as to premiums charged or plan and **only 4** percent are declined. The rate of rejection of the average Company is about 11 percent.

THIRTEENTH:—The Company issues all regular forms of policies and some not issued by any other Company. One of the latter, for instance, combines the essential features of an Ordinary Life, Limited Payment Life and Endowment.

FOURTEENTH:—All policies are protected by the Indiana Compulsory Reserve Deposit Law and carry a certificate to that effect on the face.

The Lincoln National Life Insurance Co.
FORT WAYNE, INDIANA

Good Territory Is Available In

CALIFORNIA	*ILLINOIS*	*OHIO*	*SOUTH DAKOTA*
NEBRASKA	*WEST VIRGINIA*	*NORTH DAKOTA*	*MINNESOTA*
PENNSYLVANIA	*UTAH*	*MONTANA*	*COLORADO*
NORTH CAROLINA	*IOWA*	*INDIANA*	*MICHIGAN*

Firm Foundations

After the war the largest problem at Lincoln National Life was keeping up with success. Preoccupation with internal matters characterized the immediate post-war period. In the last six months of 1918 the clerical force moved from eighty-three to ninety-five in number, and about sixty percent of the employees had served with the Company only eight months on the average. Agents were hopeful. Shepard, the Manager of Agencies, noted that "Life insurance today is the best advertised business in the country," the flu epidemic having "made the life insurance agent's arguments as to the uncertainty of life more forceful than ever before."

The home office was clearly having trouble meeting the agents' and policyholders' needs. In part, the Company's solution was the obvious one: more home office employees and a larger home office to hold them. But Franklin Mead had a radically innovative solution in mind, one which met the great influx of applications without raising costs as much as expected. This solution was lay underwriting.

In the past, underwriting, deciding whether an individual's medical, employment, and character profile merited granting him insurance, was the province of the Medical Director. Dr. Calvin H. English did it all from 1905 to 1912. After 1912 he and Mead collaborated in instituting the Lincoln's program of accepting substandard risks. In 1916 another medical doctor joined the staff to handle the increasing number of cases. Soon, Mead began to assign two female clerks, Florence Warner and Clare McDarby, the task of screening cases which involved no special impairments. Jean Pile reviewed their work before sending it to the policy issue department, referring special cases to Mead or a doctor. These women were thereby underwriters. What made them able soon to do a task previously thought assignable only to a medical doctor was a numerical rating system. This at first somewhat controversial system assigned each impairment a number of points and each favorable factor a number of credits. The sum of all the factors was the rating. Mead decided that a clerk could assess these points and credits, leaving only very special cases for the medical doctors' advice and counsel. Although women frequently performed these tasks in the early 1920s, the custom whereby marriage required a female employee to resign from the Company made it apparent that female lay underwriters' careers were too short to merit the training necessary to make them underwriters. Gradually, Mead sought only college-educated men to become underwriters. Even so, it is not difficult to see the savings that accrued from using B.A.'s rather than M.D.'s to perform the bulk of the underwriting.

Mead's importance to the Company in this and other innovative programs can be measured by his salary. He made $12,000 a year in 1920, second only to Hall's $18,000, and almost half again the amount the next most highly paid executive received (Walter Shepard's $8,500). Of course, Hall's modest salary was supplemented by the income from his special contract which brought him an extra $49,808.11 in 1921, the most he made from the contract in any year.

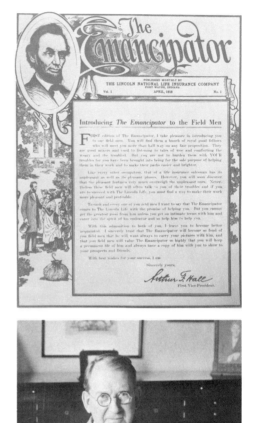

Above, the first issue of The Emancipator, *the Company's periodical for agents.*

Below, Franklin B. Mead in his office in 1930. Note the etchings on the wall behind him.

Firm Foundations

The Company went about the task of increasing office space in a similarly "scientific" way. Lincoln National Life had 219 employees in 1921. On the basis of business projections, management predicted there would be 974 employees by 1932 and 1,656 by 1937. At around 140 square feet per person, the Company would need 233,000 square feet by 1937. It was clearly time to build their own office building. The Company employed H. A. Hopf of New York, an industrial engineer, to plan for the construction of an efficient new building in 1921.

Hall favored a site well south of the center of town, at Piqua Avenue and Calhoun Street. It would allow inexpensive expansion in the future. Members of the Board favored a site downtown. Hall reported their differences frankly:

The site of the Harrison Street building before construction began.

> It has been contended by some . . . that the Company owes a duty to the community and should build a building in the nature of a monument to The Lincoln National Life and the men who are responsible for its success. It is the belief of your officers that this Company should confine itself to building a life insurance company. That by so doing it will build a great monument to the men responsible for its success and that it will fulfill all of its duties to the community if it builds a modest building in which it can carry on its activities for many years to come. This should be done at the minimum cost to secure the facilities for the Company's growing needs. The minimum of cost over a period of years can be more certainly secured on the South site than on any other site that has come under consideration.

A number of the members of the Executive Committee were downtown merchants. Led by old Samuel Foster, they overwhelmed the young Hall, and at the end of the year the Board's Executive Committee authorized the purchase of the downtown site—on Harrison Street between Douglas, Brackenridge, and the alley—for a quarter of a million dollars.

Hopf recommended a New York architect, Benjamin Wistar Morris, because it was easier for him to work with a firm based near him than with a Fort Wayne firm. Morris, who was only thirty-one years old in 1921, had graduated from Trinity College in Hartford, Connecticut, and studied architecture at the *Ecole des Beaux Arts* in Paris. His partner was Robert T. O'Conner. Although the Executive Committee invited several Fort Wayne architects and Morris to appear before them early in 1922, Morris was probably a shoo-in from the start. A three-story building on a "U" plan built with steel capable of supporting two more stories on the wings and twelve over the central unit, was agreed upon, and the Hegeman-Harris Company of New York was designated contractor. The building became an "H" with later additions to the two wings.

With the victory for the downtown site came the triumph of the monumental mentality. The first-floor lobby would be two stories high and in Grecian style. An extra $50,000 was appropriated to make this area and the plaza in front of it in keeping with the "dignity of the building, not only at its inception but especially when it would reach its ultimate proportions to the proposed horizontal and vertical extensions." The steps and plaza in front would be granite, the base artificial granite, and the superstructure Indiana limestone. The cost was approximately $1,300,000.

Hall was so happy with the work of the Hegeman-Harris contractors that he repeatedly recommended them to other insurance companies (Hegeman called Hall "our best salesman") and employed them for a $400,000 addition in 1929 without seeking proposals from anyone else. He felt that "they saved us more than their fee" by their suggestions to the architect, and, perhaps even more important to a harried member of the building committee, "they saved high salaried members of the building committee an endless amount of time." So efficient were the contractors that Hall dispensed with a building committee for the later addition and merely assigned one man, F. P. Rowland, to consult with them. Ever the good salesman, Hall sold Hegeman and Harris insurance policies and convinced them of the merit of insurance coverage of the key men in their growing firm.

The architects and the dream. From left to right, Harry A. Hopf, Benjamin W. Morris, Hall, Mead, Ninde, and John F. Bacon, an associate of Morris. The original building was supposed to grow eventually into the gigantic edifice pictured at right, but the Great Depression intervened to dash that dream.

Firm Foundations

Building the Harrison Street offices.

Few chief executive officers can resist the lures of monumentality offered in constructing the institutional embodiment of their organizational and financial labors. In May of 1922 Hall said the building under construction would be "the most beautiful life insurance building in the world." The in-house organ, *Life with the Lincoln*, explained the purity of the style:

> The classical plan of our new Home Office has not ceased with the mere adoption of pure Grecian style of architecture. Even the details of material and construction are being made to lend themselves to carry out to the limit this plan.
>
> To illustrate, the stone used is in the form of the massive stone blocks of which the ancient temples were constructed, rather than the size and shape commonly used in modern buildings. Nor is its color the pure white of the dressed limestone of today, but instead is the mottled variety that was taken from the quarries of the classical age. The effect of this coloration is a varigated one—a play of light and shadow rather than a glaring and blank whiteness.

One of the reasons Hall had favored the Piqua Avenue site was the availability of space for recreational facilities. Hall's company had a paternalistic flavor about it. In 1920 female employees had two daily periods of calesthenics conducted in the office under the direction of a YMCA employee. In 1923 Hall promoted the formation of an employees' Social and Athletic Association. The new building contained six bowling alleys for the employees. The Lincoln Life Social and Athletic Association used various recreational facilities provided by the Company: a stage with curtains and scenery for amateur theatrical events, two clay tennis courts in the rear of the building, and a driving net and nine-hole putting course for golfers on the fourth floor.

The building was dedicated on November 7, 1923. Arthur F. Hall was now President of the Company, Foster having resigned to become Chairman of the Board. It was time, Foster admitted, that Hall be first in command "in name as well as in fact." There would be "a new President to go with this building." Hall now earned $30,000 salary a year, and Shepard had pulled up even with Mead at $15,000 (but Mead received a $5,000 bonus for his 1922 reinsurance work).

Although the top management at Lincoln National Life was stable in its composition, it was not stagnant. In 1926 Alva McAndless was made Secretary of the Company, after only seven years at the Lincoln. McAndless was born in Capac, Michigan, in 1890, the eldest child and only son of Canadian parents. His father was a veterinarian, a graduate of the University of Toronto, and a man of some prominence in this small Michigan town. "Mac" (he hated the name "Alva") attended the local high school but had to take a year at nearby Port Huron High School in order to get a certificate that a college would recognize. He attended Ypsilanti Normal School briefly—just long enough to be allowed to teach in the rural schools near Capac. In 1914 he entered the University of Michigan, where he pursued a serious course of study with high distinction. Mathematics and economics were his principal interests, but he also studied political science and the German language, taking courses on Goethe, Schiller, and Lessing. Most of his grades were A's. He earned a few B's and no grades any lower. He was a member of Phi Beta Kappa.

He may have had law school in mind at the start, but J. W. Glover, a professor of actuarial mathematics, got McAndless to help him in his consulting actuarial work for Grange Life of Lansing. Alva worked for Grange Life until 1918, when he moved to the Detroit Life Insurance Company as an actuary. Common interests brought him into contact with Franklin Mead, and McAndless was employed by the Lincoln late in 1919 to become head of the Underwriting Department. Soon he was doing much of the traveling in the field for Mead's reinsurance work, and Cecil Cross took over the Underwriting Department. In 1923 he married one of Lincoln's underwriters, Maurine G. Gordon.

Moving in.

When the building was completed in 1923, Postmaster General Harry S. New came to Fort Wayne to dedicate it. New (in the fur coat) with Hall and the postal workers who turned out to greet their chief.

The completed building.

Athletics were an important part of life at the Lincoln. Hall himself (upper left) called the lines in some matches on the tennis courts behind the new offices. He left the daily calisthenics (above right) to an instructor from the YMCA, Louis Schwan. Schwan leads "physical drill" in the Policy Department in 1920. Note the tennis racquets shaped like snowshoes in the hands of the champions at right. Bowling and basketball were popular with both men and women. Hall posed with the men's bowling team (above, facing page). The women's basketball champions for 1923 are below on the facing page.

Nine-hole putting course and double driving pit atop the Harrison Street building.

Firm Foundations

Alva J. McAndless.

Though he became known throughout the industry simply as "Mac," some executives in the home office regarded him with more respect than affection. He was all business and a perfectionist. Like Mead, he retained broadly intellectual interests throughout his business life. He read widely and sprinkled his speeches at business meetings and conventions with references to Descartes and Locke. He had considerable knowledge of the history of the life insurance industry and read widely on business, economics, and politics. At one time in his life he subscribed to *Barron's Business Week,* the *Harvard Business Review,* the *Wall Street Journal, Nation's Business, Newsweek, Time,* the *Journal of Commerce,* the London *Economist, Insurance Field,* the *National Underwriter,* the *Eastern Underwriter,* the London *Monitor,* the *New Yorker,* the *Saturday Evening Post,* the *Saturday Review of Literature,* the *Atlantic Monthly, London Calling,* the *Journal of the History of Ideas,* and the *American Economic Quarterly.* His outlook on the industry and on the economy in general was broad, but he paid close attention to the details of his business. Unlike Mead, he became an avid golfer. McAndless had the sorts of talents that Hall and Mead knew how to use. He was on his way up.

Business in general was on its way up. In 1925 the Lincoln along with ten other life insurance companies completed twenty years in business. The Lincoln had eighteen millions more insurance in force than the other ten combined. Hall admitted, "I've hugged myself with satisfaction over that achievement," but repeatedly in the late '20s he warned agents and employees against complacency. He knew that the Company

The Accounting Department in 1925.

44

was riding the crest of a wave of prosperity for business in general and the life insurance industry in particular. "Since the war," he told agents in 1927, "there has not been a single business factor unfavorable to our business." He pointed to the "changed attitude of the public toward life insurance" as by far the most important factor. Everyone advertised the industry's virtues. Banks and trust companies asked borrowers how much life insurance they carried. Lawyers advised wealthy clients to buy large amounts of insurance to provide ready cash for paying inheritance taxes on their estates. Corporation stockholders insisted that key managers be heavily insured to cover the loss to the business that would result from their deaths. Partners insisted on insurance for each other. Educators told parents of bright children to buy insurance to guarantee a college education. "Since the government fixed $10,000 as the minimum amount for a soldier [in World War I], $10,000 has become a minimum standard in the minds of thousands who used to be satisfied with one or two thousand." Charles Evans Hughes, who had conducted the Armstrong investigations at the time of the Company's birth, told the Association of Life Insurance Presidents in New York in 1926 that there was no safer and better managed business in the country than life insurance. Under such conditions, Hall told his agents, of course the Lincoln was successful. He simply could not understand why those other ten companies had not done better themselves.

Miss LeDoux in the information booth in the lobby of the Harrison Street building.

The 1920s were the era of employee banquets and bonuses. Hall inaugurated the decade with a new house organ and with company "get-togethers" for the 202 employees. At the first of these meetings Hall announced plans for the new building and confessed "that I am not now having nearly as much fun working with you folks to build a great life insurance company as I used to have in the old days, when I knew everyone in the offices, and saw and talked with every one of them daily." Seven years later his theme was the same. He wanted "these offices to mean something more than just a place to work and make a living." The Lincoln Life Social and Athletic Association, the tennis courts, lounges, beautiful building, medical advice and nurses' services, cafeteria, shorter hours, and the new Personnel and Planning Department were meant to make the Lincoln "one big happy family." For three and a half years the Company had had about the same number of employees despite an ever-growing volume of business, and some of the savings in home office costs were to be passed on in bonuses ranging from five percent of salary for employees of one year's tenure to ten percent for those with ten years or more with the Company. "Our average clerical salary," he boasted in 1928, "is higher than that paid by the majority of life insurance companies." The 344 clerical workers in 1928 made an average salary of $104 a month (up from $81 in 1922). Most of them were unmarried women. Hall felt that married women could rely on their husbands' wages and should not take jobs from unmarried women or from men who had families to support. The Company's office manual stated explicity:

Firm Foundations

Arthur Hall leaves work.

Winners of a Company beauty contest in 1928. Standing, left to right: Ann Stevens, Irene Donnell, Mildred Bueter, Virginia Steinman, Genevieve Federspiel, Claire Zurbach, Evelyn Metsker, Velma Lassus, Helen Hoover, Dorothy Martin, Velda Lou Nobles. Seated, left to right: Bertha Branning, Helen Hoffman, Louise Fredrick, Bertha Knocke, Greta Astrom.

The Company has established a general policy to the effect that women employees anticipating marriage are expected to tender their resignation prior to the marriage . . .

In some few cases where circumstances warrant it, the Company may reinstate an employee resigning on account of marriage; however, such reinstatement will under no circumstances take place prior to two weeks following the marriage.

It is the general policy of the Company in reducing the clerical force, when actions arise, to terminate the services of the married women employees first.

These were standard practices among Fort Wayne's employers.

The foundations of Hall's company were firm, and it was time to think of luxuries he would never have dreamed of two decades before. Hall was serving as chairman of the Lincoln Union for northern Indiana. The Union was attempting to raise one million dollars to establish a memorial for the site of the burial of Abraham Lincoln's mother in southern Indiana. The Union employed a Disciples of Christ minister from Zionsville to speak throughout the state and help raise money for the memorial. His name was Louis Austin Warren. Hall heard him speak when Warren visited Fort Wayne and was impressed by what he saw and heard. Hall had in mind employing someone to establish something that would show the Company's debt to Abraham Lincoln. He had nothing more specific in mind, but he persuaded Warren to come with the Lincoln and establish the Lincoln Historical Research Foundation. His salary was $5,000.

Once again Arthur F. Hall proved to be a shrewd judge of men. Warren's life had not been unlike Hall's. Born in 1885 in Holden, Massachusetts, Warren was the son of an iron foundryman. His father died when he was twelve, and young Louis went to work in a grocery—fifty-five hours a week—to support his mother and younger brother. When his brother secured a better job and showed no interest in furthering his education, it was agreed that Louis would get some higher education. Influenced by a local minister, the devout Warren chose Transylvania University in Lexington, Kentucky, because it had an academy attached to it in which he could earn his high school degree. He went to Kentucky with forty dollars in his pocket, graduated from the academy in 1912, and earned a Bachelor of Theology degree four years later from the University. He founded the school newspaper, put it on a firm financial basis by soliciting advertising, and earned his way through school in part by lay preaching.

Warren's first pulpit was in Hodgenville, Kentucky, which was Abraham Lincoln's birthplace. When the local newspaper editor was drafted, he begged Warren to save his paper by editing it in his absence. Warren's congregation allowed him to moonlight, and in this way he first came into contact with questions about Hodgenville's only famous citizen, Abraham Lincoln. Wild and disturbing rumors of Lincoln's illegitimacy circulated freely in this Southern village, and Warren gradually found himself delving deeply into the "facts" of Lincoln's birth, parentage, and genealogy. He found public courthouse records on these subjects virtually untouched by professional historians. A move to Elizabethtown in 1920 brought him more county records. Eventually he compiled 550 court entries about the Lincoln and Hanks families and published his first book, *Lincoln's Parentage and Childhood* (1926). It completely reversed the rather sorry picture of Abraham Lincoln's father drawn by most previous authorities and showed him to be a skilled carpenter, a steady wage-earner, a respected middling citizen, and a responsible property-owner.

It did not take this zealot long to figure out just what the Lincoln National Life Insurance Company should do for Abraham Lincoln: it should house a substantial collection for serious scholarly research on Abraham Lincoln. Within a year Warren was already reaching out to the public with *Lincoln Lore,* a one-page weekly bulletin (such a publishing schedule seemed natural to this old newspaperman) intended as a clip-sheet to supply newspaper editors with "filler" on Abraham Lincoln. Warren was surprised to find that many people saved these throw-away sheets for future reference. The greatest private collection of Lincolniana in the country was on its way.

It was indeed a great time for establishing things. Soon, however, it would be a time to hold on to what one had.

These young women waited table at General Agents' Conference Luncheons on January 23 and 24, 1928. Top row (left to right): Evelyn Metsker, Bertha Branning, Bertha Knocke, Virginia Steinman, Claire Zurbach, Velma Lassus, Velda Nobles, and Genevieve Federspiel.

Lower row (left to right): Helen Hoffman, Louisa Fredrick, Dorothy Martin, Greta Astrom, Mildred Bueter, Irene Donnell, Ann Stevens, and Helen Hoover.

Aspirin and Austerity

By 1928 Arthur Hall could again look outward. Internally his Company family seemed to be getting along well. While McAndless was traveling around the country securing reinsurance business, he cultivated a friendship with Russell A. Norton, a vice-president of the Merchants Life Insurance Company of Des Moines. Norton was married to the only child of William A. Watts, the president of Merchants Life. Norton told McAndless that the company was for sale, and McAndless told Hall and Mead. $450 per share for 4,000 shares would secure complete ownership. Hall borrowed money from members of the Lincoln's Executive Committee, and the Company issued 50,000 shares of stock at $50 per share to stockholders or $140 per share to agents and employees. The Lincoln paid $1,800,000 for the Merchants stock and granted Watts $20,000 a year for twenty years. The Company also agreed to make Norton its loan agent in Los Angeles for ten years, with the right to lend a million dollars a year at six percent interest. President Watts saw to it thus that his son-in-law was taken care of in the transaction.

The Merchants began as an assessment association in Burlington, Iowa, in 1894—that is, members of the association were assessed to pay benefits to members who were life insurance claimants. This fraternal principal was abandoned in 1915, when the company was reorganized as a legal reserve company and took the Merchants name. In 1917 the Preferred Life Insurance Company of Grand Rapids, Michigan, William A. Watts, president, purchased the Merchants, which absorbed the Preferred Company and moved its headquarters to Des Moines. The Merchants had not been growing fast, and its agency operation was feeble. But the acquisition and reinsurance of the Merchants brought some eighty millions of insurance in force to Lincoln National Life—an attractive gain for a Company bent on having a billion dollars of insurance in force by 1930. The only strong agency gained in the transaction was the Grand Rapids, Michigan, agency of A. G. ("Bert") Green.

Meanwhile, Warren was hard at work carving out his corner in the growing Fort Wayne company. Repaying the Company's "debt" to Abraham Lincoln was entirely Hall's idea. "Every one of the officers had to be sold on the proposition," Warren recalled. Some were downright hostile to this seemingly frivolous foundation; others tolerated it as the President's hobby. But Warren was a formidable salesman as well as a Lincoln scholar. He quickly realized that there could be no research on Lincoln without a library and archive on which to base it. The library of Judge Daniel Fish of Minneapolis, one of the "Big Five" Lincoln collectors who had dominated the field of collecting Lincolniana for decades, was available. Within two years of his arrival in Fort Wayne, Warren convinced the Company to purchase the collection for about $40,000. Shrewdly, Warren also realized that Fish had not been an active collector for over a decade and that there was, therefore, a big gap in Fish's holdings. He obtained the collection of Albert H. Griffith of Fisk, Wisconsin, a younger collector, to fill the gap. Then, showing considerable entrepreneurial ability of his own, the preacher-turned-Lincoln-scholar sold the duplicates in Griffith's collection for about $5,000. $4,000 of this sum he used to purchase L. E. Dicke's collection

Daniel Fish was one of the "Big Five," who dominated Lincoln collecting around the turn of the century. This handsome bookplate identified the books in his collection.

Aspirin and Austerity

Louis A. Warren reads one of his great early "finds," a small campaign biography of Lincoln written by Reuben Vose and published in 1860. Warren holds one of only two copies of the work known to exist.

of Lincoln prints, an invaluable group of some 1,500 lithographed and engraved pictures of Lincoln. This transaction proved to be the model for Warren's operation for years to come. In 1935 he established the Lincolniana Publishers, which purchased books and pamphlets, retained the items not already in the Lincoln Historical Research Foundation, and sold the duplicates at a profit. These profits provided the acquisitions budget for future Foundation purchases. In this way, Warren built and maintained one of the greatest collections of Lincolniana in the United States at no cost to the Company except his own salary and operating expenses and the initial purchase price of the Fish and Griffith collections.

At a meeting of the Company's agents at the home office on January 11, 1929, Hall explained his role as President. He was "to think and plan for the future," freed now by his capable organization from the personal supervision of the Company that had been his task until about 1919. What he was thinking about now was reducing the cost of insurance. The Company needed legislation to allow it to lower its premiums by valuing the business in a new way. The Company needed changes in the Indiana investment laws governing life insurance—"the most archaic and strict of all our 48 states." Office costs, already showing a healthy trend downward over the last six years, needed reduction, and so did agents' costs.

In the summer Hall fought an attempt by the Company's largest stockholder to sell control of Lincoln National Life to interests in New York or Chicago. He was quite sure that the stockholder could not secure control: "I truly believe that I am the only one who could do it, and I have twice refused a million dollars to use my influence for such a purpose." Hall took "as much pride in having organized and guided this company to its present proportions and success as I do take in the development of my children." He could not conceive of "any influence" that would make him take such a step. In 1930 he repeated what would become a standard litany: "There is no use for any one to talk about the Lincoln Life leaving Fort Wayne." Allen County residents held most of the stock and "would not consent to it under any conceivable condition." "For one thing," he added, "the clerical costs here are at least 35% less than they are in Chicago or New York."

By Christmas, Hall was thinking about bewildering new problems. "The only stock that is not down is Bayers Aspirin," he said. Like most businessmen, he was worried about the stock market crash of that year. True, the Great Depression was not quite the calamity for the life insurance industry that it was for other industries, especially in states like Indiana with lenient insurance departments which allowed companies to stay in business by showing worthless assets at high values. But it caused plenty of headaches.

The most obvious area of difficulty was income from investments. The state of Indiana did liberalize the law governing insurance investments in 1929. Previously limited to U.S., state, and municipal bonds; notes secured by first mortgages on real estate; policy loans; certificates of deposit; and collateral loans secured by investments otherwise sanctioned, the Company's investors could now seek industrial bonds and common and preferred stocks.

At the beginning of the Depression, the Lincoln's investment portfolio showed the effects of the history of restriction. As a 1927 report put it:

> The investment laws of the State of Indiana do not give a life insurance company very much latitude as to investment. It permits of first mortgage loans and bonds of such a selective class that they are very hard to obtain, and therefore, it is almost necessary for a life company incorporated under the laws of this State to confine the investments to mortgage loans in order to secure an adequate investment yield.

Except for the investments inherited from Michigan State Life and Pioneer Life, Lincoln National Life put its money substantially in mortgage loan investments. From 1912 through 1920 this policy had gained the Company an average of 5.4% earnings.

In the investment area and there only, the 1920s foretold the bleak future. In 1919 the Company made what were probably its first foreclosures—thirteen of them. The decline was steady through the next two decades. By World War II, the Company had acquired almost $35 million worth of real estate. Nevertheless, investments in mortgages increased throughout the 'twenties; they reached over $49 million by 1931. Municipal bonds and government bonds in the decade offered 3-1/2% to 5% yields, but mortgages on farms and ranches were more attractive. Besides, this was a Midwestern company which had put its faith in the virtues of rural life for keeping its mortality low.

Warren (above) was jaunty and affable, but he was also a dedicated student who had given up the ministry for Lincoln. The Lincoln Historical Research Foundation (left) was a haven for scholars and, in Warren's view, almost a temple for paying respect to Abraham Lincoln, America's patron saint.

The home office viewed from the south in the late 1920s.

Daniel B. Ninde.

The Lincoln was a life insurance company not a real estate company, and ownership of farms and ranches was not the Company's desire. Hall, Mead, Ninde, and McAndless were not farmers, nor did they want to be. In fact, hardly anyone wanted to be a farmer in the agriculturally depressed 1920s—hence all the foreclosures on farms and ranches for want of ability to pay what was due on their mortgages. By 1928 the Lincoln's executives, not wanting to don overalls and grab pitchforks, finally began to look to investment pastures that were not literally green. Almost a million dollars went into bonds in that year. Over a million went for bonds the next year, and (reflecting the latitude of the new Indiana law) $142,500 bought Shell and Anaconda stocks. In 1930 over four million dollars worth of bonds and stocks came to the Lincoln. But it was too late.

Early in the decade of the 'twenties the Company hoped to sell the foreclosed properties. By 1924, however, it was clear that no one wanted to buy them. Hall explained what happened to the Insurance Department examiners three years later:

During the last few years we have been obliged to foreclose on a considerable number of mortgage loans and have thereby acquired a number of farm properties. At the time of acquiral there was no market for farm properties and we were consequently obliged to hold them. The question arose as to the best method of handling these properties as it was found in a considerable number of cases that the soil, although good at the time the loan was made, had become impoverished and fertilization was necessary. It became immediately evident that some money must be spent on them, if they were to be put in a salable condition and kept that way until there was again a market for farms. In the opinion of our Finance Committee the best way to accomplish these results was to stock the farms with cattle. In this way the land would be fertilized and the cattle would serve as a medium for the consumption of such crops as could be raised. Also, it was hoped that there might be some profit from the stock operations.

The farms were located in Indiana, Michigan, and Ohio. They baffled the Indiana insurance examiners. The Company, the examiners said in 1927, "for its own use, prepared a figure that would indicate that it had made a small profit in the purchase and sale of livestock."

> However, [the report continued] there are so many things to be taken into consideration with the feeding of livestock, such as charges to the cattle for use of the farms, feed produced by the farms, incidental labor, charges for interest on money used to purchase cattle, and various other items which are hard to definitely allocate, and on the other side, cattle are probably entitled to a credit for the fertilizer of the farm, so as may be seen, it is impossible for either the company or the examiners to arrive at a definite conclusion as to the advisability of this method of operating farms.

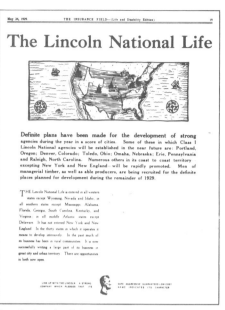

On the brink of the Great Depression, the Company looked hopefully to expansion into new cities. It had not yet entered business in New England, New York, much of the Southeast, or the more sparsely settled states of the West.

Leaving for the agency convention in Quebec in 1930.

Aspirin and Austerity

May 24, 1929.   THE INSURANCE FIELD—(Life and Disability Edition)   18

The Lincoln National Life

The Lincoln National Life Insurance Company, after a period of testing and experimentation, has just placed in the hands of its agents a remarkable new, copyrighted policy which makes an unusual appeal to business men and to large buyers of insurance. During the month of March the average size of policy written on this contract was $14,650. The momentum is just starting on this specialty which offers, in a form that is exceedingly flexible, permanent protection at lowest cost. Contracts of Twenty-Five, Fifty and Hundred Thousand size are coming in rapidly from all parts of the country. To develop this contract in accordance with its potentialities will require immediately the addition of a considerable number of strong men to The Lincoln National organization.

THE Emancipator policy, popular and successful as it is, is but a leader in the strong line of The Lincoln National. The strength of its multi-optioned, Twenty-three Year Endowment contract, its Endowment Annuity at Sixty-five and its Preferred Risk contracts has been proven by years of sturdy experience in the field. The Lincoln National Life has a complete range of policies to supplement its splendid specialties.

LINK UP WITH THE LINCOLN   A STRONG
COMPANY WHICH PLEDGES THAT ITS   SAFE   AGGRESSIVE GUARANTEED-LOW-COST
                                             NAME INDICATES ITS CHARACTER

"Link-up-with-the-Lincoln," said this advertisement which boasted of a new policy which averaged $14,650 in coverage each sale.

There was high comedy in another Lincoln National Life agricultural experiment, the growing and distilling of mint. Mint had the virtue of compactness in its liquid state, and it sold for thirty dollars per pound—when the project started. By the time the Company treasurer's safe held enough of the fragrant essence to give the halls of the building a pleasant, minty aroma, however, the price fell to three dollars. After 1928 the whole project of operating farms was abandoned. The Lincoln decided to take its losses on the farms. Hall commented with considerable understatement in 1930: "We didn't start our strenuous campaign for the sale of farms any too soon."

One can chuckle in retrospect, but there was a forecast of tragedy in the Lincoln's disastrous investment experience. There was personal tragedy, too. Daniel B. Ninde, one of the Company's founders, was head of the Investment Department. The examiners in 1927 not only scratched their heads over problems of measuring cow manure as an asset but also at the state of the Investment Department's records in general, which were inadequate for an examination. Franklin Mead had extolled the virtues of the rural Midwest in the past, but he caught on quickly: the investments must be diversified. In 1930 Ninde left the Company. Mead was given $25,000 for special services from 1927-1930, doubtless for straightening out the confusion in the Investment Department.

The life insurance industry as a whole invested heavily in real estate mortgages in the 1920s, but the Lincoln far exceeded the industry average. In 1920 the Lincoln's real estate mortgages more than doubled the average percentage of assets so invested in the industry, and even by 1935, it exceeded the industry average (23.1%) by 6%.

For the insurance industry, investments were the principal problem posed by the Depression, but they were not the only problem. As Alva McAndless explained to an industrial insurers' conference in September of 1931, a depression also increases underwriting costs. Agents submitted increasingly unsatisfactory business for the home office's approval. Agents had trouble maintaining their own income and were therefore less selective, and "persons with impaired finances" were easily sold. Such insurance prospects, their income shrinking from the opulence of the 1920s and their estates threatened with shrinkage, applied for substantial amounts of insurance to protect their families. The Lincoln's rejection rate rose 30% in 1930 from the 1928 level. In 1931, measured by dollar amounts of business rejected, the rate was 75% higher than the 1928 level (6% to 3.3%).

Suicides—and suicides disguised as accidents—became a major problem. In the 1920s suicides accounted for 5% of the Company's death claim losses. In 1929, even though the disastrous decline in prices was not well under way until October, suicides accounted for 11% of the losses. McAndless saw clearly that the detectable fault in these bad risks was overinsurance, and he wanted his agents and underwriters to ask the question "to what amount of insurance is a man with a given income entitled?" Recent experience showed that potential suicides were most often men who wished to reimburse those who had trusted them with their money. He warned underwriters to watch out for bankers, public administrators, administrators of charitable institutions, husbands who had lost the property of wealthy wives, and sons who had been repeatedly financed by wealthy parents. Beneficiaries named were not only wives and dependent children but also brothers and others who had given the insured some financial support in his life. The Lincoln's losses had been incurred particularly on real estate developers, country bankers, and stock brokers. McAndless wanted the suicide exemption extended from one to two years. Income disability coverage, which caused at least one insurance company to fail, also needed restriction. Moreover, the large policies (called "jumbo risks") taken in the prosperous 1920s, from the Lincoln's experience, simply were not paying off; too many people were loading up with insurance in anticipation of proximate death.

Doctors Harry Martin and Glenn English found Shirley Temple, one of the Company's famous policyholders, physically fit.

The buoyant Hall remained optimistic—or at least maintained a public image of optimism. In October, 1931 he explained to a board member who had indicated an intention to resign, "that following a depression the life insurance business booms, and I am expecting the next five years to be the greatest in the history of the business." Not only politicians thought prosperity just around the corner. Besides, Hall added, "Expenses of all kinds have been cut to the bone." Company officers had taken salary cuts of from 15% to 27% for the year. Investments were changing too. Hall looked hopefully at loans to and ownership of Kansas City apartment houses.

Hall was concerned about the Company's investments, of course. In 1931 the American Founders Corporation of New York purchased a substantial amount of Lincoln Life stock. American Founders was an investment, not a management, company, but the election of American Founders vice-president George E. Devendorf, manager of their investment department, to the Lincoln's board in 1930, was widely interpreted as a move to strengthen the investment advice the Lincoln received. W. W. Zachary of American Founders was elected to the board in 1931. Zachary and Hall were both keen on increasing the amount the Company invested in stocks, and both hoped that the Indiana law limiting such investments to ten percent of total assets could be changed.

Aspirin and Austerity

Helen Lewis and Vera Mueller, secretaries in the Investment Department in 1929.

Investment problems aside, there was still money to be made in life insurance, and Hall knew just how much.

> Our regular business [he told a correspondent in a letter marked "Strictly personal and confidential"] gives us a net loss of $12.00 a thousand for the first year and an annual profit afterwards of $3.50. Thus it takes four years to overcome the loss and at the end of the five years a thousand dollars of regular business has earned us only $5.50.

> Reinsurance costs us a net deficit of $3.65 a thousand the first year but returns an annual profit thereafter of $3.00 a thousand, thus in five years a thousand dollars of yearly renewable term insurance has earned us $11.35 net as compared with only $5.50 net on regular business.

> We do not want other companies to know the large profit we make on reinsurance. Many complications might arise. Other companies might enter the business in competition with us, or we might find it necessary to reduce rates.

The key to the Lincoln's success still lay in that early move into reinsurance. At the end of 1929 the Company had $386,763,000 of term business reinsured from three hundred other companies. In the five years before 1930, Hall pointed out, "our earnings on reinsurance have been greater than on our other insurance."

Hall would have been even more confident had Herbert Hoover won reelection to the presidency in 1932. Hall was "more stirred by this presidential election than by any other in my lifetime." The choice was simple, he told local political leaders in a circular letter on his own, not the Company's letterhead: "Either we go ahead with the recovery now beginning or we risk delay of recovery for two or three years."

> To me, Hoover has had the toughest presidency since Lincoln. . . . Throw him out now, tear down everything he has been building, let Congress devote a year or two to debate, and we will have nothing short of a catastrophe.

> I am personally talking to people who are in doubt about this election. I have set my mark to get five of them pledged to support the President at the polls. I am picking THREE out of the five from friends of mine who have lost their jobs or their businesses. And I am asking five of my friends to do what I am doing—go out and get five votes.

> If you feel at all as I do as to the tremendous importance of this election to the country, I wish you would do this, too:

> 1. Go out personally and get five doubtful votes pledged to the President, in particular seeing those friends of yours who are without employment, to whom an overthrow of the government means an added and needless year of distress, and—

> 2. Ask five of your friends to do the same thing I'm asking you to do. The one way to a save this situation is for every man of us to go to work personally, and not ask the President to carry our load for us.

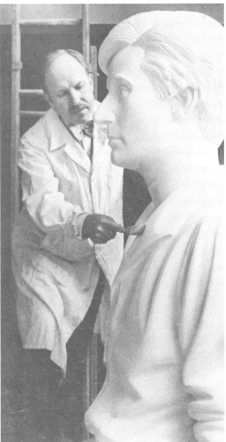

From its inception, the Harrison Street building was meant to have a statue in the plaza. By 1928 the Company was planning a memorial to Lincoln, celebrating his youth in Indiana (1816-1830). For sculptor Paul Manship this was a challenge. Lincoln left Indiana when he was twenty-one years old, and there are no photographs of him before he was thirty-seven. Louis Warren took Manship on a tour of the country associated with Lincoln's youth, and the sculptor found that "Lincoln's childhood excited the imagination. [Carl] Sandburg's books and talks with Ida Tarbell vivified my impressions which led to the desire to represent the youth as a dreamer and a poet, rather than the material aspect of the railsplitter. . . . Without these qualities of spirit, the idealism and clarity of his future visions would never have been possible."

An air of excited anticipation attended the preliminaries of the unveiling of Paul Manship's statue—as well it should have. Manship was one of twentieth-century America's great sculptors. Born in St. Paul, Minnesota, in 1885, he moved to New York City in 1905. Study in Rome led him to appreciate Renaissance sculpture and ancient Greek art. He received numerous important commissions but was famed especially for his reliefs. Louis Warren recalls that knowledgeable people were as interested in the four medallions at the base of Manship's statue as in the statue itself. Manship executed the reliefs on New York's Western Union Building and the J. P. Morgan relief memorial for the Metropolitan Museum of Art before moving his studio to Paris in 1922. He returned to New York five years later. Not long after his work for the Lincoln National Life, Manship completed his most famous commissions, the Paul J. Rainey Memorial Gateway for the Bronx Zoo and the Prometheus Fountain at Rockefeller Center.

*"Abraham Lincoln, The Hoosier Youth"
was unveiled at ceremonies held on
September 16, 1932. Numerous famous
people were in attendance, including
Dan Beard, a founder of the Boy Scouts
of America (upper left), and Manship
himself (with Arthur Hall, upper right).
The sculptor confessed to "a mortal fear
of such occasions" and said very little.*

Ida Tarbell (at left with Louis Warren), journalist and author of numerous Lincoln books, came to Fort Wayne for the dedication of Manship's statue. The featured speaker was Arthur M. Hyde, the Secretary of Agriculture. Arthur F. Hall, III, the Company President's grandson, pulled the cord that unveiled the statue. Manship was paid $75,000. The dedication ceremonies cost $35,000.

Aspirin and Austerity

By 1935 the Lincoln had had the worst of its Depression experience. The Company anticipated at least $2,000,000 more in losses on mortgage investments, to be distributed over the next several years. From 1929 to 1935 assets increased yearly, dividends were paid each year, only 1933 showed a decrease in surplus, and insurance in force had increased despite increased lapses. The number of employees was fairly stable, around 650 throughout the 1930s (the ratio of women to men was about 2:1 in 1929). During the Depression the ratio of women to men fell to about 5:4, proof that Hall continued to protect the jobs of men with families to support. The average clerical salary in 1932 was $105.50 a month. Turnover was low (down from 22.7% in 1929 to a mere .7% in 1932) since clerks held on to their precious jobs in these bad times. The few new clerks in the Lincoln, all of them honor students, began work at a $40 a month salary.

Companies that were weathering the Depression less well fell prey to the healthier ones. The Company seized the opportunity to acquire several other companies (thereby keeping its insurance in force on the rise). In 1932, for example, the Lincoln purchased and reinsured the Northern States Life Insurance Company of Hammond, Indiana (in receivership) and the Old Line Life Insurance Company of Lincoln, Nebraska. A year later it acquired the Royal Union Life Insurance Company of Des Moines (also in receivership). These bold acquisitions helped keep the Lincoln's amount of insurance in force from declining in the early Depression years.

The stockholders were clearly uppermost in the minds of the Lincoln's management. The dividends were 25% of par in 1930, 1931, 1932, and 1933 and 16% in 1934, 1935, 1936, 1937, and 1938 (they went up thereafter). As Hall knew only too well, the stockholders had to be satisfied. Many of them were right in Allen County looking over his shoulder. In fact, some substantial stockholders were officers in the company. The Lincoln spread its losses over a long period, paid its dividends, reached out boldly to hold the line against shrinkage of business in force, and looked hopefully to a better future.

Billboard advertising in the 1930s featured interpretations of Lincoln by some of America's greatest illustrators.

Part of the Agency Department in 1929.

Austerity and Aspiration: The McAndless Era

From the beginning Arthur F. Hall was careful to avoid making Lincoln National Life a one-man company. Franklin Mead was Hall's logical successor, but he died suddenly in 1933 at the age of fifty-eight. Thereafter, Alva McAndless was the most likely man to succeed Hall. In 1938 Hall learned that he had serious heart trouble. In the fall he announced his intention to become Chairman of the Board. At the annual meeting in February of the next year, McAndless became President.

At the time when McAndless (left) took over from the aging Hall, the Company finally reached a billion of insurance in force.

McAndless was well prepared for the job. In addition to Hall's careful grooming by exposure to many facets of the business, McAndless benefitted from his own wide reading. His speeches to agencies and national actuarial societies alike were sprinkled liberally with references to Lord Chesterfield, Descartes, Carlyle, and Buckle. He apparently read some of John Maynard Keynes' works. He was a firm believer that the liberal arts were good training for business. He felt "strongly" that his "usefulness was very little determined by such practical techniques" as he "mastered in college." The liberal arts were good training for original thinking, and even salesmen could benefit from the *entree* liberal learning gave to good business prospects. Though hardly a fan of government intervention in the economy and national economic planning, the trend towards which he recognized, he was nevertheless realistically convinced that the "right of regulation and supervision is well founded."

Before becoming chief executive officer, McAndless mastered the investment side of the Company's operations. This was still an area of grave concern. Speaking to general agents in 1938, McAndless noted that government bonds, which yielded only about 2% interest, were useful only for "idle funds." The Company's premiums were calculated on the assumption that investments would yield 3%. Railroads, in which the Lincoln invested only 7% of its assets as opposed to as much as 33% ~ 66% for some large Eastern companies, were in a "sad plight." Heavily regulated and facing severe competition from trucks, this industry offered little opportunity for investment. The government largely preempted rural real estate credit. Besides, the Company had been burned by such investments before. Mortgage loans on city property, mostly homes rather than businesses, were the most hopeful field, and to that the Company turned increasingly in the late '30s and early '40s. Utilities offered attractive investment opportunities as well, but many insurance companies were bidding for their debt. The Lincoln had 11% of its portfolio in utilities in 1938. Both railroads and utilities required very lengthy obligations, thirty years usually, and McAndless disliked such risks. The American economy changed too rapidly, McAndless thought, to make those areas very attractive.

Hall congratulates A. L. Dern, Director of Agencies, on the occasion of reaching a billion dollars of insurance in force.

The year McAndless became President, the Company reached its long-sought goal of a billion dollars of life insurance in force. New business was not a problem. The problem was low interest rates, and this would continue to be a serious problem which would occupy the officers' thinking for a decade. And there were the uncertainties of another war on the horizon.

In December of 1940 interest on government bonds reached a new low, 1.9%. McAndless blamed the low rates, not on the government, but on gold. He argued that the United States was fast coming into ownership of most of the gold in the world, and its plentiful presence made money plentiful as well. Because of declining interest rates, the Company had had to change its rates for insurance in 1937. At that time, the officers considered emphasizing participating policies, which distribute a share of the company's profits in the form of dividends to policyholders. They decided against it then, but early in 1941 they got the board to amend the Company's charter to allow a major increase in participating business. McAndless thought it essential to allow the Company to pass interest losses on to the consumer as well as losses from unanticipated taxes. The latter he considered a significant threat with war in the offing. Gone were the days, he explained to stockholders in 1941, when the Company could get over a crisis by taking a subscription from the stockholders, as it had in 1918-1919 with a $300,000 subscription to cover the losses from the influenza epidemic. You will get smaller margins of profit, he told them, but you will get a certain profit. McAndless, schooled in the hardships of the Depression years, was adept at handling austerity.

Like all good chief executive officers, McAndless had considerable ability to predict the future. New business increased only one percent in 1940, and that increase was due primarily to reinsurance business, still the Lincoln's great strength. Regular business had declined, in part because the Company restricted amounts of insurance it would accept on men liable to military service. This was a year after war started in Europe, but it was a full year before America's involvement in the conflict. The Company's expertise in reinsurance, on the other hand, was reaping substantial dividends. Thirty percent of the Lincoln's increase in reinsurance business in 1940 came from new connections with four large Eastern insurance companies.

A decrease in the Company's lapse rate accounted for more revenue than new business, a feature McAndless attributed to the country's improving economy and to the selection of better agents. Since the lapse rate fell by 8% on reinsurance and by only 6% on ordinary business, however, the economy must have been the major factor, for reinsurance, of course, was not sold by Lincoln agents.

Although already anticipating war, McAndless was by no means fearful of the future. Again, his wide reading—especially his knowledge of international economic developments—served the new President in good stead here. Mortality losses in World War I, McAndless knew, did not destroy a single great German insurance company; inflation did it.

Interest rates seemed uppermost in McAndless's mind. With top quality public utility bonds yielding 2.6% in 1940 and the Company's rates premised on an assumption of higher rates than that, the Lincoln turned heavily to federally insured F.H.A. mortgages. It had $52 million in mortgages, and well over half ($29,196,000) were in F.H.A. loans (yielding 4.17% interest). Conventional mortgages ($22,665,000) yielded 4.56% on city property and 4.64% on rural.

The Lincoln's overhead seemed high to stockholders. But, McAndless assured them, this was an illusion. Reinsurance, which was the most important part of the Company's business, required a highly-paid technical staff. Best's reported the Company "more expense-minded today than ever before," and McAndless boasted that the report stated that "Expenses are remarkably low." The Company's overhead was high, too, for a reason McAndless did not report to the stockholders. Optimistic that the Lincoln would survive to do business in better days, Hall and the other officers had apparently taken the view during the

New business on September 23, 1935 —300 applications for approximately one million dollars of insurance.

Depression that the staff would be valuable again one day. Reductions in staff had been minimal. Employees during the Depression had the eerie feeling that there was not enough work to go around, and some junior management performed tasks not much above the clerical level. The Lincoln's Depression-era acquisitions, some felt, were aimed as much at getting work for the staff to do as they were at reaching that elusive billion-dollar goal. On the brink of World War II, the Company had 571 employees in the home office, 151 branch-office employees, and 922 full-time agents.

As the struggle in Europe deepened and America's involvement became more certain every day, Hall was having his own personal struggle —with death. The doctors who diagnosed Hall's illness advised him that if he gave up golf, late hours at the office, and cigarettes he could prolong his life a good deal; otherwise, they gave him only three years to live. Hall enjoyed life and continued to live it the way he always had. Photographs taken late in his life show him on the golf course with his characteristic cigarette holder in hand. Life style meant a great deal to this man, an elegant dresser who sported a white Van Dyke beard. It even affected his politics. In 1930 he had joined the board of directors of The Association Against the Prohibition Amendment. He continued to work in the office until the spring of 1942, a sign that McAndless did not make all the decisions for the Company in his early years as President.

Hall's decision to continue life as usual was deliberate, and his children never heard him express regrets about it. He suffered a mild stroke in the winter of 1941-1942. Even after he was confined to his home, he kept his Company family in mind. He scheduled a series of brief interviews with all the Company's employees who had served ten years. Each came to his house. Hall often awaited them in the garden. A nurse

Advertising often reflects the political and social concerns of an era. This ad, published six months before the bombing of Pearl Harbor, capitalized on the prevailing concern for America's preparedness for war.

An aging Arthur Hall weighs in for a physical examination. The results were not good.

greeted each caller and warned him to hold the conference to twenty minutes' length. To each caller he said something different, usually something to help their careers. To Henry Rood, a young actuary with the Company, he told how he had groomed a man to become President of Lincoln National Life. That man (probably McAndless) had come to the Company as rather a stiff actuary, prone to seeing everything in black and white. Gradually, Hall saw to his involvement in various community affairs, broadening him and humanizing him. Under Hall's guidance he came to see the virtues of opinions that fell in gray areas between black and white. When Rood went home, he suddenly realized that the story was a parable, meant to guide him, also something of a stiff and legalistic actuary, in his future career.

Hall was an Episcopalian, a vestryman active in the church's financial affairs. But he was not an active church-goer. As the end grew nearer, he apparently sought some assurance about his future state. An unsigned carbon copy of a letter to Hall of July 28, 1942, mentions "the assurance you have received from your minister concerning your standing before the Lord of Creation." The unnamed correspondent went on:

> Throughout your years you have drunk deeply of life as it is lived in the world of affairs. The end result of your efforts is the Lincoln Life, whose hundreds of thousands of policyholders and thousands of agents and employees have enjoyed and continue to enjoy life in greater abundance than would have been possible except for that company. Surely this attainment alone—forgetting the innumerable contributions you have made in other directions in the interest of human welfare—justifies your assurance and knowledge that you have lived a Christian life in truth and in fact.

On December 9, 1942, Arthur F. Hall died.

McAndless had to face the problems of World War II without Hall's guidance. Remembering the previous war, McAndless feared war itself less than "an epidemic which sometimes follows as a sequel to war." He established a $400,000 contingency reserve to meet unforeseen circumstances. He knew, too, that labor costs would be a special problem and workers hard to get. In 1941 the Company had to increase starting clerical salaries and grant a cost-of-living bonus at year's end to maintain adequate personnel.

McAndless worried about the threat of taxation. He argued repeatedly that the insurance industry made an important contribution to the war effort by keeping inflation down. The industry in general and the Company in particular increased investments in government bonds. In 1942, for example, almost 60% of the Company's increase in bond holdings was in government bonds. By diverting people's savings, in the form of insurance premiums, to the government, the Company thus reduced the amount of money consumers used to pursue scarce goods in the tight war economy, McAndless argued. The Company made other contributions as well. Eighty-five men from the field and thirty-five from the home office were in military service in 1942; forty-two of the former and eleven of the latter were officers.

War, like depression, was not the calamity for the insurance industry that it was for other sectors of the economy. The Company wrote more new business in 1942 than in any year except the peak years of 1929 and 1930. Home office staff fell from a high of 640 in 1941 to 556 in 1942. The decrease caused a lengthening of the work week and increased clerical salaries. The tight labor market led to the abolition of the ban on married female employees (the ratio of women to men grew to 3.1 by 1948). Mortality experience, despite war, was good. It rose only slightly in 1942. Improvement came particularly in the area of accidental deaths (which resulted in double indemnity payments). Accidents (and faked accidents) were a feature of the Depression. The economic basis of suicide and recklessness was gone, and so was a great deal of automobile

This 1942 advertisement linked life insurance and the war effort with a somewhat strained connection between political and financial freedom.

The beautiful original doorways to the Harrison Street building, since altered, carried plaques between them with the names of Lincoln National Life servicemen during the war.

driving with the scarcity of fuel. Reduced driving and reduced speed, as always, reduced accidents. And, as was so often the case with the insurance industry in the twentieth century, medical advancements decreased mortality. Sulfa drugs in "the last few years," McAndless reported in 1942, had led to a "remarkable" decrease in deaths from disease. Since most soldiers were young men without families, McAndless noted, they were men without life insurance, and the war had little effect on mortality. McAndless considered the chance of bombing in America remote and noted that even in England the bombing had not drastically increased mortality.

Taxation, however, was not to be avoided. The Company would pay a federal income tax for the first time in ten years in 1943, McAndless stated. He estimated the tax at $135,000, and, characteristically, explained the history of taxation in the insurance industry:

We shall nobly save or meanly
lose the last best hope of earth

—ABRAHAM LINCOLN

LINCOLN pleaded that if the cause of freedom was lost in America it was doomed everywhere.

Now this nation, which more than once has protected and preserved the liberties of the individual, stands again as "the last best hope of earth." And never before in history have our people joined together so singleheartedly for defense of our institutions.

Not everyone can serve on the fighting fronts—but all can serve by saving; all can invest in war stamps and war bonds; all can help conserve the things America needs to win!

Saving is the vital thing, whether you do it directly or through an insurance company if you require financial protection. The Lincoln National Life Insurance Company cordially extends its services to help the American public with such plans.

More Than A Billion Dollars Of Insurance In Force

THE LINCOLN NATIONAL LIFE
INSURANCE COMPANY

FORT WAYNE, INDIANA

ITS   NAME   INDICATES   ITS   CHARACTER

This 1943 advertisement doubtless pleased President McAndless, who argued that the life insurance industry contributed to the war effort by diverting savings into war bonds that might otherwise pursue scarce consumer goods and cause inflation.

The Company was exempt from tax because of the Federal method for taxing life insurance companies. Only a very few companies had to pay a tax during this period. This situation existed because the law relating to the taxation of life insurance companies provided that they should be taxed upon the basis of their interest income in excess of the theoretical interest necessary to maintain the reserves. Because of a reduction in interest rates and because of heavy investment expense due to large holdings of real estate, the companies as a whole were not earning a net rate of interest which brought about the imposition of a tax. There was another reason why life insurance companies escaped taxation. In addition to having a deduction for the theoretical interest necessary to maintain reserves, they were allowed to deduct from their total interest income the interest from tax-exempt securities. In effect, they had a double deduction for interest on a portion of their funds. The Treasury, faced with great war expenditures and recognizing that life insurance companies under this formula were receiving certain advantages which were not accorded to other financial institutions, early in 1942 proposed to the life insurance business a change in the method of taxation which would result in revenue for the Treasury. In its early negotiations with the company representatives, the Treasury stated that they recognized the social importance of life insurance and therefore did not want to unduly burden the business with taxes and, secondly, the Treasury recognized that life insurance companies as such could not be a major source of revenue. In consequence of such a statement of position, it was not difficult to work out with the Treasury a plan for taxing life insurance companies— not burdensomely, yet on a basis within the capacity of the business to pay.

McAndless's ability to predict the future, though far short of perfect, remained substantial. In October of 1942, he predicted that the war would be over in 1943. This proved wrong, of course, but in May of 1943 he predicted that the war would last into 1945. He had predicted "the coupon economy" as well. He predicted increased controls on the economy and an increasing market for life insurance in the lower middle-income stratum of population, as labor improved its lot and the wealthy faced diminished incomes from taxation. He did not think the country was "doing so well as we should" on the question of financing the war effort. "There is not a readiness of our people to take fiscal punishment and to bury deep and permanent the bogy of 'inflation,'" he said. The only correct policy was "heavy taxation and the purchase of bonds out of current savings." Thirty percent of America's expenditures came from taxation; England was raising 50-1/2% by taxation. He was hopeful that war would develop a vast foreign trade area for America.

An index of McAndless's independent thinking was his deep interest in Russia. Some of his ideas were startling indeed for an American

Employees were encouraged to invest in government bonds to support the war effort.

business executive. In a letter to R. Nelson Snider, written on August 19, 1942, McAndless expressed his interest in "the question of private control of rights in land vs. nationalization of rights in land."

> . . . in the densely settled countries there is much to be said in favor of nationalization of rights in land. A very interesting topic along this line would be a history of the utilization of land in Russia. There is much misunderstanding regarding collective farming in Russia. The land problem in Russia has arisen out of serfdom, the muzhik land holdings under the Czar's regime, and collectivization under the Soviet Republics. With our Anglo-Saxon standards, we criticize. Perhaps what they are doing is for the improvement of agriculture in Russia, and the changes which already have been made indicate the dependence of a state upon the peasant land holders.

Not so unconventional was his interest in races and racialism. He thought race "ties into the underlying causal philosophy of all history."

> The Teutons probably have carried this philosophy into nationalism to a greater degree than any other people; they hold that in any group of men there is not only an individual leader but subservient to him there is an aristocracy of leadership, and a monopoly of these qualities in their own particular race.

No Bolshevik would have recognized a fellow traveler in McAndless. This sturdy capitalist had no liking for the doctrines of Karl Marx, though he had apparently read "The Communist Manifesto." He was, however, a forward-looking businessman. He admired individualism and private enterprise, but his speeches lacked the rhetoric of *laissez-faire*. He saw private industry as "definitely threatened in the thirties," but he thought "its phenomenal wartime attainments" had given it "another chance to prove its right to survive." Private industry's "principal opponent" was "its gigantic self," he said. He repeatedly stated that insurance "is essentially social in nature." He faulted the industry for failing to reach "the lower income levels of the population." He saw definite possibilities for group insurance in this area, a feeling coming to be held by many industry executives who saw group benefits grow in importance during the war when the government froze wages. McAndless's 1945 statement to the stockholders for the first time mentioned group insurance, though Lincoln had been selling small amounts of it for several years. The group field would grow in importance after the war, especially after the 1947 Taft-Hartley Act recognized group benefits as a subject of collective bargaining between labor and management.

In one other respect McAndless was somewhat atypical. The son of Canadian parents, he had a cosmopolitan outlook. The English and Canadian economies always interested him, and he tried to profit by their experiences. He took a dim view of nationalism, a name which merely "dignified" the traditional "relation of strife" which prevailed "between national groups" in a long and "disenchanting" history of "eternal conflict." He despised this "order of the jungle" with its "assertion of a national ego without regard for the rights and interests of other national groups." He praised "the concept of international cooperation."

McAndless had great hopes for sales. He remembered vividly the situation after the First World War, when hoarded money, bank accounts, and war bonds quickly began to pursue consumer goods and life insurance. Ordinary sales had almost doubled in 1919 and nearly trebled by the end of 1920. After a brief period of adjustment at the termination of this war, McAndless expected to see a similar boom in life insurance sales. Still, sales would not be automatic. It seemed to be a time to stress agency development, which had been weak at the Lincoln. Reinsurance, of which the ordinary agents tended to be a bit suspicious if not jealous, had "provided the profit margins out of which we develop our direct business," McAndless told his agents in 1944. "The real objective of the institution today is to build a direct-writing agency force which will produce bona fide business with a profit margin in it." McAndless kept his speeches to salesmen brief. He began one speech at an agency meeting by saying, "This is not a pep meeting; it is a business meeting. Cross and Dern will open the inspiration spigot later." He seemed more at home describing interest trends and predicting the future of the American economy.

The interest trends McAndless foresaw were anything but favorable. Early in 1946 he predicted that premiums would soon have to be premised on the assumption of 2-1/2% interest rates. The Company continued to invest about 2/3 of its increases in investments in government bonds at 2-1/4 to 2-1/2% interest. Investing heavily in mortgages to counterbalance it did not work because many capital-rich corporations were pursuing the boom in building after the war.

McAndless breathed a sigh of relief when the war was over, admitting that some of his statements during the late Depression and the war had been more optimistic than the facts warranted; the ship's captain, he explained, had to keep the crew's morale up. On the whole, the Company and the industry had handled the war well. Promptly inserting war exemptions in its new policies, the Company had worried only about older policies which lacked them. There were enough of these to be troublesome, since some of the Lincoln's strongest agencies were in towns with large air force bases and since the relatively young agency force had sold policies to relatively young men. The war brought about $4,000,000 in increased mortality claims which were balanced substantially by the greatly decreased civilian mortality during the war. Now, McAndless saw prosperity ahead. America was becoming a nation of employees, workers in skilled crafts and in white-collar jobs, rather than a nation of small proprietors and independent farmers. Seventy percent of the national income now went to the employee group, and they passed equity to their heirs not in a small enterprise or pieces of land but in life insurance. Though runaway inflation, which erodes confidence in life insurance, was greatly to be feared, McAndless knew that "we seem to profit out of a gradual inflationary trend." Gradually rising costs of living made people feel their insurance protection was inadequate, and they sought to increase it. Moreover, sulfa drugs, penicillin, blood plasma, and blood albumen were making great inroads on mortality rates.

McAndless was a President whose views were shaped by a period of austerity. He was a reserve-builder. He was tight-fisted with dividends to stockholders. As he explained to stockholders in 1949, "A reason for building very large surplus is the desire to place the Company in a very strong financial position so that it may take advantages of unusual opportunities for profits as they arise." Having built reserves for emergencies, McAndless was now building reserves for opportunities. And one of the reasons he wanted a capital-rich corporation stemmed from a disappointment he had experienced during the Depression. Then, the Life and Casualty Company of Nashville, Tennessee, had been for sale for a very small amount of money. McAndless wanted the Lincoln to acquire it, but even that small amount was unavailable in the dark days of the Depression. He wanted that never to happen again.

In 1951 McAndless, who watched the family-owned corporations closely for aging owners who might want to sell out, thought he saw his opportunity in the Gulf Life of Jacksonville, Florida, an industrial insurance company owned by T. T. and E. E. Phillips. T. T. Phillips died, and his brother spoke to McAndless of selling the company. McAndless spoke at the agency conventions that spring of buying a company. He dispatched Actuary Henry Rood, lawyer Clyde Cover, and the Reinsurance Department's John Phelps to Florida. They asked Mr. Phillips about the price. He said he wanted $35,000,000. They said they thought the price too high. Phillips replied, "Well, then, put on your hats and go back to Fort Wayne." The Lincoln's negotiators then hemmed and hawed, said they were only the technicians to evaluate the company, and told him that he and McAndless would have to negotiate the sale. Mollified by this, Phillips let them talk to his lawyer and his actuary. A contract was prepared.

Later, in Fort Wayne, Henry Curry, an officer of the Mellon National Bank and Trust Company of Pittsburgh dropped by to see Rood. He said that McAndless, whom he had come to see, was out of the office; he would like to get acquainted with some of the other officers. Rood invited him up to his office. The Mellon Bank had acquired the Farmers Bank, which owned the Reliance Life Insurance Company of Pittsburgh. The Bank Holding Act forbade national banks to own insurance companies. The Mellon Bank would have to do something with the Reliance—sell it, turn it into a mutual company, or divide the stock among the Mellon Bank's stockholders. When McAndless returned to the office the next day, Rood told him about his conversation.

McAndless contacted John Mayer, the new president of Reliance Life. Preliminary negotiations showed that the Bank had five years to do something about the Reliance. They were in no hurry, therefore, and they were interested in finding a purchaser that fulfilled three conditions. First, the purchaser had to be a company of integrity which would run the Reliance well. Second, the purchaser must agree to treat the employees of the Reliance decently. The Bank felt a responsibility towards the many people who had worked for the insurance company for a long while. Third, the purchaser would have to pay a fair price. Rood knew the Lincoln could fulfill those demands, and he thought the Company could easily pay $20,000,000-$30,000,000 in cash. The Mellon Bank was ready to deal.

The Reliance Life Insurance Company, named for an America's Cup yacht, was founded in 1903. Always controlled by bankers, it was a more conservative institution than the Lincoln. After a spectacular start, it grew slowly and steadily, having $1,066,000,000 of insurance in force by 1951 by contrast with the Lincoln's $4,255,000,000. The Reliance never went in for acquiring other insurance companies. It took the route of the slow development of a strong agency force. Its agencies were expensive but productive. It was a sound company—a plum, in fact.

Gulf Life was forgotten, and negotiations with the Pittsburgh company occupied most of the summer of 1951. They began at the plush Duquesne Club in Pittsburgh, one of those old-fashioned big-city gentlemen's clubs, with a blizzard of white cloth hand towels in the washrooms and Frederick Remington bronzes in the halls. McAndless, Cover, and Rood were the first negotiators. The Reliance men supplied them with documents indicating the Company's condition. Back home in Fort Wayne the Lincoln's Board of Directors authorized McAndless to purchase the Reliance at a price not to exceed $30,000,000. For the next meeting in Pittsburgh, Ed Auer accompanied Rood and Cover; Auer had a reputation around the Company (and the Company's suppliers in Fort Wayne) for being a very tough negotiator. McAndless, however, feared that Auer might be a little too tough, and he saw to it that he and Rood were the principal negotiators. The process of arriving at a price began with a $20,000,000 offer. The Reliance bargainers suggested that the value of the agency force must be added to that as well as the value of new business written since the first of the year and other items. The figure reached $26,500,000, and Rood was satisfied at that point that the Reliance negotiators had tacked on to the original bid just about everything that they could dream up. The Reliance men still groped for further additions. Suddenly, McAndless, who had been silent to this point, said, "Well let's settle the thing for 27-1/2 million." Rood could not believe his ears. He never knew whether

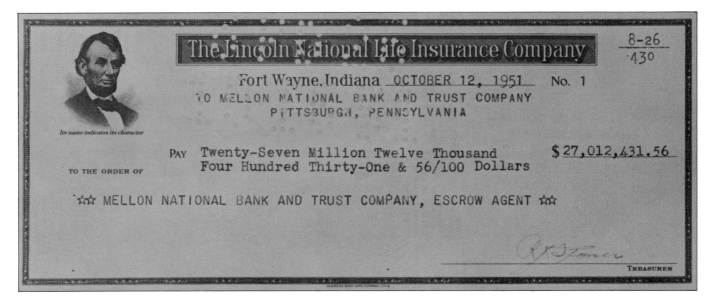

McAndless had been somewhat inattentive and thought the bidding was at 27-1/2 million or whether he felt impatient with the haggling and wanted to sweep the details aside with a top offer of one million more. The Reliance negotiators agreed to recommend the figure to the Mellon Bank's officers.

The fact of the matter was that McAndless, the surplus-builder who had devoted most of his career at the Lincoln to caution and austerity, at last had a chance to ensure prosperity, and he was not about to miss it. The Mellon Bank accepted the offer. The rest of the transaction involved dealing with a mass of details and trying to keep the transaction secret until fully consummated. The latter was a difficult task, but it was done successfully. Only one "insider" benefitted. A shrewd secretary at the Mellon Bank overheard two vice-presidents discussing the sale to Lincoln National Life. She went immediately to her broker and bought Reliance stock. The event led to a Securities and Exchange Commission investigation, but she was allowed to keep her profits on the grounds that she had not been a principal of the transaction.

Throughout the transaction the Mellon Bank had been exceedingly solicitous of the interests of the Reliance's employees. Over a period of five years, the Pittsburgh Company was essentially absorbed by the Lincoln. Every employee was offered a job in Fort Wayne at his current

*McAndless in his office,
decorated with Daumier cartoons.*

salary or better, an offer that could be made because most of the married female employees and young unmarried female employees would not move. Likewise, the Lincoln accepted the Reliance's agents' contracts. This would not have been possible and would probably have blocked the sale had Mayer, in one of his first actions as president of the Reliance, not scaled down the rather high commissions the Reliance agents were used to receiving. The Lincoln acquired an extremely valuable agency force which repeatedly had individual and agency leaders in the Lincoln's sales thereafter. The sturdy Baltimore, Birmingham, and Cleveland agencies and a generally strong presence in the South, not previously an area of strength for the Lincoln, became big assets.

The Lincoln's officers knew there was money to be made in the transaction. In the first place, the bankers who had controlled the Reliance had always invested extremely conservatively. Most of their investments were in low-yielding bonds, and the Lincoln's men knew that they could improve the portfolio. In the second place, the Reliance was a rather high-expense company, and the Lincoln executives were confident that they could improve efficiency in the operation. These improvements would be profitable bonuses for acquiring a bloc of sound business at a fair price. And the Reliance's home-office staff supplied numerous valuable additions to the Lincoln's staff, including a future head of the Marketing Department, Jack Rawles, and a future Medical Director, Dr. Harry Cochran.

McAndless's enormous accomplishments as President of the Lincoln have been somewhat obscured by his one-man management style, a style totally out of keeping with recent management philosophy and a style which caused considerable wriggling among the Company's managers in his own day. He was friendly enough with the clerks and line managers, many of whom remember him fondly. The higher management, however, remember him differently. It was often said of him that he could sit at any desk in the Company and perform the job well—a feat which is not even a goal of modern business executives ever wary of too much involvement in "details." McAndless frequently appeared in the departments, leaned over a worker's shoulder, and asked the worker what he was doing. The clomp of his cleated shoes usually gave enough warning that the departments appeared to be models of orderly diligence. Nevertheless, nervous managers usually rushed to the worker in question as soon as McAndless left the room.

Managers who developed a tendency to arrive at work later and later in the morning usually found their secretaries telling them that McAndless had been by to see them at 8:00. Some managers felt constrained to come into the office on Saturday to be sure McAndless saw them there. As soon as he left for home, so did they. He loved to play cards, but, fearing that it might set a bad example for the employees, he never played in the office. When he had a trip to make, however, he sometimes skipped lunch so that he could get on the train early and start playing cards. He seemed not to know what an organization chart was. McAndless liked to drop by offices, visit with the staff, and solve a problem or give an assignment right then and there—no matter whether he gave

Dr. Warren in the
Lincoln Library and Museum.

the assignment to a junior executive without telling his boss. Sometimes, he handed out assignments this way that had customarily been the boss's work, much to the awkward embarrassment of the junior executive.

There is no gain saying the fact that McAndless was simply tight with the Company's money. Personally, he was anything but greedy or tight, but the office was another matter. Because of his Canadian background, he never took much interest in the Company's growing Lincoln Collection. His speeches rarely mentioned or quoted from the man after whom the Company was named. When he did take a role in the Library and Museum's affairs it was usually with an eye to saving money. When Louis Warren got wind of a unique bronze Lincoln statuette by famed sculptor Truman Bartlett in an antique shop in Baltimore, the asking price was $800. Warren wanted the money. On a business trip, McAndless dropped into the shop and posed as a collector of Lincoln statuettes to decorate his (non-existent) vacation lodge. He looked at the Bartlett statuette and offered the proprietor an insulting $300. That proved to be McAndless's top figure. Warren let the statuette go, but his successor acquired it years later, when the Company had a new chief executive officer.

Workers from the McAndless era tend to remember episodes like these, but it would be a serious mistake to let them crowd out of the picture his tremendous accomplishments. He was an exemplar of learning, economic sophistication, and realistic business reasoning. His fabulous memory for names endeared him to all the clerks. His careful management of the Company in the last years of the Depression and through the war compares favorably with that of any large insurance company's chief executive officer. And his willingness and readiness to purchase the Reliance when the opportunity came launched the Lincoln National Life Insurance Company into the modern era.

The Bartlett statuette.

77

Alva McAndless (center) at golf.

New Directions

The Reliance acquisition marked the end of the McAndless era. Ironically, what McAndless had done by acquiring the large company in Pittsburgh was to make his own management style obsolete. If it had ever truly been possible for him to perform every job in the Company, it was no longer true in the early 1950s. The Lincoln was a giant corporation, selling group and health as well as life insurance, and no one could master all the details of the operation. No one could afford to ignore the organization chart now. McAndless continued to make his regular visits to the offices of the Company's executives, but the visits were shorter and less comfortable. His answers to questions seemed abrupt.

In January of 1954, McAndless faced a rigorous schedule of agency conventions, two in Florida and two in New Orleans. In the golf rounds with agents customary at these gatherings, McAndless did not play very well. He complained of fatigue. He rose early, as usual, on Monday, January 24th, and had two or three breakfasts in the hotel dining room with different agency groups. He addressed a meeting that morning and, after lunch, went to play golf with three agents. After the 12th or 13th hole, he felt too tired to continue and started to walk back to the club house. He collapsed on the course. His golfmates got a taxi for him and called a doctor. The doctor said that he should go to the hospital. McAndless insisted on being taken to the hotel instead. A flustered agent telephoned Walter Menge to ask him what to do. Menge advised him to follow the doctor's advice, ignore McAndless's wishes, and Menge would accept the responsibility. At 7:30 p.m., McAndless died of a heart attack in a hospital room.

A special board meeting was held the next Friday. Thirty seconds after the question of selecting a new President was presented, the board elected Walter Menge by acclamation. Had the Company needed a new President seven years before, it would likely have been Leland "Pete" Kalmbach, but he left the Company in 1947. As always, there were those in 1954 who thought they had a chance for the job and really did not, and rumors focused particularly on Louis Reitz, then head of the Reinsurance Department. Reitz, however, was a member of the board at the time of Menge's election, voted for Menge, and promised him his cooperation. Nevertheless, three months after the board meeting, Reitz left the Company.

Walter O. Menge was born in Buffalo, New York, in 1904. He moved with his family to Detroit at an early age. Of German-Lutheran stock, Menge's father was a wood-carver and a member of a union. The Menges owned their home in Detroit but were hardly well to do. Menge began working in the eighth grade, first on a newspaper route and then in a grocery store. Later, he worked summers in the office of the American Auto Body Trimming Company. After graduating from Detroit's Eastern High School, Walter attended Detroit Junior College (now Wayne State University), for want of funds to go to a better school. He took engineering courses, but a wise mathematics teacher noted his abilities in that field and suggested studying actuarial science. In 1923 he entered the University of Michigan as a junior. He worked nights

Walter O. Menge.

collecting dry cleaning from the fraternity houses where the wealthier boys lived. After his first semester he became an assistant in the statistical laboratory of the University.

Menge graduated in 1925 and earned a masters degree the next year, teaching mathematics part time while he studied. In 1926 he became Actuary for the Grange Life Insurance Company in Lansing. In 1928 he returned to Ann Arbor to teach actuarial science. Three years later he earned a Ph.D. In 1937 he joined the Lincoln National Life Insurance Company. He had long been acquainted with McAndless, who gave him his choice of jobs, Underwriting or Actuarial Department. Menge made a wise choice. Figuring he already knew quite a lot about actuarial problems, he chose what he did not know, underwriting. McAndless gave him no appointed task in the department; Menge was to carve out a job of his own making. Essentially, he entered at the top, working from the start on large and interesting problems, studying substandard rates, helping revise the rate book, investigating exclusion riders connected with aviation, and devising a hospitalization plan for the Company's employees. He took charge of the Lincoln's important reinsurance operation in 1947 when Kalmbach left. Four years later he played a large role in managing the Reliance acquisition, and McAndless made him president of the Reliance during the transition from Pittsburgh to Fort Wayne. He was the Company's First Vice President when McAndless died and was his likely successor, though McAndless had made him no promises.

Menge inherited a thriving company. In 1956 the Group Department reached the one-billion-in-force mark. A year later the board authorized expansion of the home office building to bring all the Company's employees under one roof (as the Lincoln expanded, it had been forced to use temporary office space in other locations than the building Hall had erected on Harrison Street). The addition was dedicated in 1960, bringing over twice the floor space available before the construction. Mere physical expansion was a shortsighted solution to a growing work force, and the board also authorized in that year the planning for use of computers to diminish the volume of clerical work.

Reinsurance continued to constitute an important part of the Company's business. Competition in this line had increased since the war with the entry of many American companies into this specialized market and the return of the German companies, but there was still plenty of business to go around. Between 1949 and 1955 the number of legal reserve life insurance companies in the United States nearly doubled. The proliferation of small new companies provided a sustained demand for reinsurance on policies above their necessarily modest risk-retention levels. These companies also needed the specialized underwriting a reinsurer would provide for substandard risks but which a small company could not afford. Oddly enough, Menge pointed out, reinsurers helped these new companies, competitors for ordinary business, because the success of the companies would mean a continued demand for reinsurance services. With $7-1/2 billions of insurance in force in 1956, the Lincoln was the ninth largest insurance company in the United States.

This rank proved hard to maintain. Companies with larger group departments grew faster. No big opportunity like the Reliance acquisition came along and already in 1957 the Lincoln had fallen to tenth place. To remain competitive, the Lincoln introduced a new ratebook in 1957 which reflected a loosening of restrictions by state insurance commissioners. Previously, many had required charging the same premium rate for each $1000 of insurance. Since the costs of handling a policy of any size were relatively fixed, it was to the Company's interest to offer lower rates for larger policies. This, the new ratebook did. Menge called the book "not only progressive, but aggressive." Menge hoped to stimulate direct sales. In 1956 the Company introduced the President's Trophy to be awarded to the general agent who did the best job of recruiting agents each year. He increased the national advertising budget. But an actuary, temperamentally unsuited to marketing, headed the Agency Department.

Two years after Menge became President, Dr. Warren retired as Director of the Company's Lincoln Library and Museum. He was seventy-one years old and the only head the institution had had in its twenty-eight-year history. Replacing this amiable collection-builder, public speaker, writer, and general ambassador-without-portfolio for Lincoln was no easy matter. But back in the early days of the Foundation, Warren had employed a promising young college graduate in the Lincoln Library and Museum, R. Gerald McMurtry.

President Menge explains the Reliance acquisition.

R. Gerald McMurtry as a youthful apprentice in the Lincoln Library and Museum in the 1930s.

McMurtry had been in Warren's Sunday School class in Kentucky years before and had corresponded with the older man about historical questions. In 1932 he leaped at Warren's offer of a job. It was the depths of the Depression, and McMurtry was grateful to find work. For two years McMurtry lived alone in Fort Wayne, first at the YMCA and then at the University Club, and dreaded the lonely weekends and holidays away from the absorbing work with the historical collection and the wonderful public contacts such a job gives. McMurtry learned how to handle a Lincoln collection in this brief apprenticeship and did some research and writing. His first work at the Lincoln, *The Lincolns in Elizabethtown, Kentucky,* chronicled Abraham Lincoln's contacts with McMurtry's hometown, and his second, *Lincoln Knew Shakespeare,* came to be widely used and helped establish McMurtry's continuing interest in Abraham Lincoln's acquaintance with literature.

The "smell of printer's ink" was intoxicating, but the salary was only $100 a month. That had looked fine when McMurtry had been a year and a half without work, an eager college graduate (Centre, 1929) looking for his first job. But he married a Fort Wayne girl, and he needed a more substantial income. Warren told him that there was no chance to raise the Foundation budget for such a purpose, and McMurtry left in 1935 to sell insurance in his mother's agency in Elizabethtown. This was not a wise choice because, he found, the potential clients who called him always wanted to show him old books from their attics or talk about history; they never wanted to discuss insurance. In 1937 Stewart W. McClelland, the president of Lincoln Memorial University in Harrogate, Tennessee, who had met McMurtry on a visit to the Fort Wayne collection, hired him to establish the university's Lincoln collection.

From 1937 to 1956 McMurtry built a fine collection, by far the best Lincoln collection in the South, and developed a special knack for collecting. He had a powerful command of the enormous Lincoln bibliography and was somehow often in the right place when a great rarity became available. Gradually, he became acquainted with most of the great Lincoln scholars and collectors, particularly through his editorship of the *Lincoln Herald,* a quarterly journal published at Harrogate and devoted exclusively to articles on Abraham Lincoln.

In the early 1950s a constant subject of speculation when Lincoln students got together was, what was the Lincoln Life going to do when Warren retired? The common answer was that the Company would simply close the place when Warren left, so inextricably was Warren's personal reputation tied up with this collection. The scholars underestimated the Fort Wayne company. Warren began to seek applicants for the job. Many applied, but McMurtry, happy with his job in Harrogate, did not. A number of people in the field, however, suggested to Warren that McMurtry was the right man for the job. After two trips to Fort Wayne in 1955, McMurtry decided to make the move.

McMurtry *was* the right man for the job. He had a genial personality, he knew how to collect, he was an experienced writer (by 1958 he had written numerous books, pamphlets, and magazine articles, most of them on Lincoln), and he had experience as a public speaker. Above all, he had the important quality (which he shared with Warren) of complete absorption in the subject. The chance associations of his youth—his birth in the town where Lincoln's parents first set up housekeeping, his residence as a boy on the same piece of land where Lincoln's stepmother lived, and his personal acquaintance with descendants of Kentuckians who were friends and neighbors of the Lincolns—gave him the feeling that studying Lincoln's life, collecting Lincolniana, and spreading the word about Lincoln were about the most important things a man could do. His interests were different from Warren's in some particulars. McMurtry had little interest in genealogy, and he was much more interested in museum relics and memorabilia. But different interests served the Lincoln Library and Museum well by leading to the strengthening of its collections in areas other than those Warren stressed. Though himself a lover of all kinds of manuscript and printed materials, McMurtry made the greatest strides toward collecting materials suitable for museum display; whereas Warren had invisioned the institution primarily as a research collection.

The guard changes at the Lincoln Library and Museum. McMurtry (left) and Warren shake hands.

Headquarters of the Dominion Life Assurance Company in Waterloo.

Menge continued the tradition of acquiring other companies that sold insurance. In January of 1957 the Lincoln purchased control of the stock of the Dominion Life Assurance Company of Waterloo, Ontario. Canada had an expanding economy with an expanding insurance market, a stable government, and a very sound currency. The Lincoln wanted a part of that market, but the experience of other American companies operating directly in Canada had not been good. Nascent Canadian nationalism dictated indirect participation through a Canadian company, even though it broke the Lincoln tradition of reinsuring the business of companies it purchased. The transaction was markedly different from the acquisition of the Reliance. The Mellon Bank had worried about price, soundness of the buyer, and the future treatment

Walter O. Menge (right) with A. S. Upton, President and Managing Director of the Dominion Life Assurance Company (left), and Ford S. Kumpf, past President of the Dominion, at the time of the Lincoln's acquisition of the Canadian company.

of the Pittsburgh company's policyholders, agents, and home office workers. Remembering that experience, the Lincoln's negotiators stressed the Company's ability and willingness to treat the Dominion employees and policyholders well. In this case though, the seller cared about one thing and one thing only: price.

Menge was a learned corporation president, more scholarly in a disciplined sense than McAndless. If anything, he was less a salesman than his predecessor. His speeches, even to agencies, were models of lucid prose and tight organization, containing occasional pieces of dry wit. Shy, reserved, stately in appearance, and gentlemanly, he was not an inspirational speaker, but he worked for improvement. Pencilled notes at the top of an early speech by Menge cautioned: "slow loud emphasize smile." Menge knew that the Lincoln was much too large a company to run in the manner McAndless had. He was a great delegator, and the executives enjoyed their new freedom under Menge. One of the first problems he faced after assuming the presidency in 1954 was a lack of depth in the organization. McAndless's lack of interest in organization and the proliferation of new insurance companies made good, young, promotable managers hard to find. Menge insisted that each department head develop a capable successor for his own job (ten years later, he noted that the strong ones chose strong successors and the weak ones, weak successors). He recognized that McAndless's cost-conscious austerity did not fit the 1950s. Most who worked for him agree that he loosened the reins a bit.

The Dominion purchase was characteristic of Menge's solutions to the Company's problems. Throughout his presidency, he had a capital-rich corporation which was faced with lackluster direct sales of ordinary life insurance and declining relative position in the industry. Reinsurance was the Lincoln's great strength, and Menge's reputation for technical expertise and integrity fit perfectly with the Company's image as an insurer of insurers. He gave due emphasis to the reinsurance operation, but his solution to other marketing problems was essentially to seek new markets. In 1956 Menge admitted that "The plain facts are that in 1955 our direct agencies, in the aggregate, fell behind the general pace of the industry." He stressed recruiting in the agencies. Thirteen percent of new direct business, he pointed out, came from new agents within a year of the inception of their contracts. If 13% of an agency's business did not come from that source, Menge told the general agents, then the agency was behind in recruiting. The Company spent an average of $644 on fringes and conventions for each agent each year, Menge reminded them, and that ought to be some inducement to new recruits. Nevertheless, from 1957 to 1962 sales of ordinary life in the United States were stable despite population growth and growth in Gross National Product. The Lincoln's performance was dismally below average for the industry. In 1962, for example, the volume of ordinary business written directly by Lincoln agents fell 1% in premiums and 7% in volume from the previous year. Menge repeatedly reminded general agents that the Company was slipping in this area.

The cupola atop the Harrison Street building comes down to make way for the 1960 addition to the home office.

The home office of American States, in Indianapolis.

Menge added new agencies and sought a new head of the Agency Department, but his principal strategy was indirect: he sought new markets. The Canadian market was the first. Next came New York. In 1960 the Company formed a subsidiary in the Empire State to tap this large and lucrative market. Two years later the Lincoln acquired a majority interest in the American States Insurance Company of Indianapolis, the largest non-life insurance company in Indiana.

The mix of reasons for acquiring American States typified the Lincoln's approach to problems in the Menge era. In part, it was meant to be a solution to the marketing problem. Though Menge was not sure how the industry would develop, he wanted the Company to be in a position of readiness should it turn out that "one-stop" all-lines marketing was the wave of the future. With a large and successful property-casualty company as a subsidiary, the Lincoln would not be caught unprepared if the industry headed in the "one-stop" direction. Moreover, Menge, along with other life insurance executives, had decided that it was not economically desirable to work the broad life insurance market of small policies and high lapse rates (what used to be called before the 'sixties the "blue-collar market"). Since practically everyone has to have property-casualty insurance, however, the American States was a way to tap this market to some degree through agents whose entire livelihood did not depend on commissions from life insurance sales. As was often the case with the Lincoln, there was an important reason to acquire the American States for the sake of the Lincoln's reinsurance business. Despite increased competition since the Second World War, the Lincoln was the largest life reinsurer in the world. Much of the competition came from European companies which offered their clients reinsurance in all lines of business. Recently, the General Reinsurance Corporation, America's largest professional non-life reinsurer, had formed a life reinsurance affiliate. "If we are to keep property reinsurance companies with life affiliates from proselyting our life reinsurance clients in these foreign areas," Menge warned, "it is necessary that we be able to offer all lines of coverage also." Finally, of course, Menge was convinced that profits could be made from property-casualty business despite its occasional periods of difficulty with claims. And he was right: the American States proved to be spectacularly profitable.

Within less than a year of gaining control of American States, The Lincoln National Life Insurance Company sought its first direct access to the European market by forming (in September of 1963) the Compagnie de Reassurance Nord-Atlantique (CORENA), an all-lines reinsurance company which operated in Western Europe and was soon to move into the African and Asian markets. Those international horizons dimly perceived by McAndless at the time of World War II had proved not to be far away at all.

Menge began to refer to "the Lincoln family of companies" in his speeches, and it was clear that the nature of the Lincoln was changing. He formed a committee to study establishing a holding company. It may have brought some uneasiness among the ordinary life agents of the parent Company, and Menge felt called upon to explain that the vast reinsurance operation did not harm them. To some, it may have appeared that the Lincoln's reinsurance operation simply encouraged the life insurance agent's competition. Without the financial aid and technical underwriting assistance supplied by reinsurers, it seemed, the many small new companies that were appearing could not survive. That might be so, Menge replied, but economic opportunity was the American way, to refuse to deal with them would constitute an illegal boycott, and the new companies would simply turn to another reinsurer. He argued for a broader view. The successful reinsurance operation helped the agents by increasing the Company's overall size and prestige. It helped, too, by developing knowledge of underwriting, especially in research on substandard cases.

Despite these efforts, the Lincoln's standing in the industry as a whole was slipping in terms of insurance in force. After regaining ninth place after 1957, the Company fell to tenth in size among American life insurance companies in 1962. It was growing, of course, but it was growing at a rate slower than some other companies in the industry. Menge never blinked this factor away, and he used it repeatedly as a goad to what he called "an agonizing reappraisal of agency development."

In 1964 Menge became Chairman of the Board, in part because of difficulties he had with a tight-fisted director who was a holdover from the more austere McAndless era, and Henry F. Rood became the Lincoln's President, a move Menge made in keeping with his earlier demands on department heads. He had picked his successor too.

Henry Rood was born in 1906 in Port Chester, New York, the son of a Yale graduate and civil engineer. Henry's grandparents were Congregationalist missionaries, and he had a pious upbringing. After his father died in 1914, Henry moved with his family to New Haven, Connecticut, where he attended public high school. He worked at various odd jobs as a youth. He received a B.A. from Oberlin College in 1928 and a Master's degree from the University of Michigan a year later. Walter

CORENA headquarters in Paris.

New Directions

Presidents, even when they are dignified actuaries, are inevitably involved in the high-jinks of sales promotion campaigns. The "cowboy" is Henry F. Rood.

Filipino Lincoln agents.

Menge was his professor in one of his graduate courses at Michigan. Shortly after graduation in 1924, Rood went to work for the Travelers Insurance Company. When the Depression came, prospects for raises and advancement looked poor, and Rood decided to seek employment with The Lincoln National Life Insurance Company. He began work in Fort Wayne in 1931 in the Reinsurance Department and moved to the Actuarial Department in 1935.

Rood worked regularly on the annual financial report and performed various other special assignments often given to him on McAndless's casual visits to his office. In 1943 he joined the Navy and worked in the Requirements Review Division of the Secretary of the Navy's office. He returned to Fort Wayne in 1946 and quickly assumed the title of Actuary. He worked on the new rate book issued in the late 1940s and was one of the principal negotiators in the acquisition of the Reliance. Afterwards, Menge took charge of the agency side of the Reliance's operations and Rood handled the home office side. He commuted regularly to Pittsburgh, spending four days a week there and one in Fort Wayne.

A tireless worker and a fast walker and talker, Rood impressed his superiors with his technical abilities in the life insurance business, and he was closely associated with the Reliance acquisition, the Company's most important venture in decades. He had high hopes for the future, but he was so near Menge's age that he felt that he would never become President because he and Menge would retire at about the same time. Late in 1962, however, Menge indicated that he would like to lighten his management load, share more responsibilities with Rood, and eventually make Rood President.

When Rood assumed the top position in 1964, he envisioned the Lincoln's becoming "not only . . . a great life insurance company but . . . a great financial institution." He thought the Company might well become principally a holding company which controlled many different financial

institutions whose products would be marketed by diverse specialists through the agency system. He looked forward to the Company's becoming a "financial department store." In this respect, Rood was quite like Menge, though, if anything, he was more enamored of the move away from the domestic life insurance market than Menge.

In 1965 the Lincoln founded the Lincoln Philippine Life Insurance Company, a hedge against nationalization in a market where the Company had operated for some time. In the same year it established the Dominion-Lincoln Assurance Company, Ltd., to reach a new market in Britain. Life insurance in England was customarily sold by lawyers, bankers, and brokers. British companies rarely operated an expensive agency system. Naturally, the market tended to consist of the well-to-do people who frequent the offices of lawyers and bankers. Canadian and Australian companies operating in England, however, had become successful in reaching the broader middle-class market through an agency system. Menge and Rood hoped to copy these companies and reach that market as well.

Rood and Menge relished the opportunities to reshape the Lincoln in the direction of a financial holding company something like Trans-America Corporation, but without diversifying into manufacturing and other product lines. Personnel problems were more vexing to both Menge and Rood, technicians more adept at handling numbers than people. Unlike marketing and financial questions, however, personnel questions often cannot be shelved pending further study. Ambitious young executives were too impatient for that.

Rood was fifty-eight years old when he became President and knew that he could not long postpone the designation and training of a new management team for the Lincoln. It was a problem born of simple demographics. In the Depression the Company had not hired many new people. As a result, most of the top executives by the early 1960s were near Rood's age or a little older. The same group had run the Company for at least two decades, but something had to be done for the future. Rood began by considering who his successor should be. He jotted notes listing the pros and cons of the top candidates, rating them on a scale of 1 to 10.

Suddenly, this planning seemed very important. Rood suffered a heart attack in a Florida airport. As soon as he began to recover, he thought of those notes about the future chief executive officer locked up in a file in his office and saw to their recovery. Menge, who was enjoying retirement, agreed to stand in for Rood, coming into the office every other week. He promised Rood to see the crisis through, but he would not stay in the office one day longer than necessary. He also promised to defer all long-term decisions until Rood came back.

Rood began to come back into the office for short periods early in the spring of 1967. Rood, fearing that he might have another attack from which he might not return, moved quickly to make clear who his successor would be. He chose Thomas A. Watson. In 1968 Rood became Chairman of the Board but he remained the chief executive officer until he retired in 1971.

Gordon Reeves, Henry Rood, and Sam Adams sign documents to form Lincoln National Corporation.

Today Lincoln National Corporation is listed on the New York Stock Exchange.

Today Lincoln National Corporation is listed on the Midwest Stock Exchange.

In 1968 Rood realized Menge's and his vision by forming Lincoln National Corporation, a holding company that would become the parent corporation of Lincoln National Life and all the other corporations the Company had been acquiring and establishing since Menge became President. Rood became Chairman of the Board of LNC and made Gordon C. Reeves, the principal legal architect of the holding company, President. This gave the Company new flexibility in acquiring other companies because insurance laws limited the percentage of assets an insurance company could invest in one kind of operation.

A year later Lincoln National Corporation gained control of Chicago Title and Trust Company, engaged in title insurance and (through subsidiaries) in investment banking, record storage systems, and microfilm and computer services. Lincoln National Corporation put the Fort Wayne Company's stock on the New York Stock Exchange listing for the first time and brought substantial federal regulation through the Securities and Exchange Commission for the first time.

Henry Rood was obviously an extension of Lincoln tradition. He was schooled in the Company's affairs under McAndless. He was in all essential areas thoroughly of the same expansive frame of mind as Menge. Like McAndless and Menge, he was an actuary trained at the University of Michigan. Rood's successor, however, clearly was a break with this tradition, and it is to Rood's credit that he was willing to change the tradition the Company had apparently established in selecting its chief executive officers. Rood felt that any manufacturing company, for example, should have high-ranking officers skilled in different areas of operation critical to the success of the business: a financial specialist, a production specialist, and a marketing specialist. He felt that a company should rotate its presidency among executives with these different specialties. A corporation like the Atlantic & Pacific Tea Company,

President Rood (left) and the headquarters of the Chicago Title and Trust Company.

which relied too long on a production specialist to head the company when it began to stress its own production of grocery products, allowed its marketing responsibilities to be slighted, kept its small stores in downtown areas while other chains built larger outlets in suburban shopping centers, and came to grief.

What Watson had always thought would keep him from consideration for the presidency in fact became his greatest asset. He had not followed what appeared to be the usual route to success in the Company's high management. He had never worked in the Reinsurance Department, and he was not an actuary or a graduate of the University of Michigan. But, in Rood's eyes he was a capable administrator. Personally generous, Watson was adept at watching the Company's expenses. He worked most of his career in the Group Department, where margins were smaller than in the other departments. He consistently recommended lower annual salary increases than other departments and still retained the necessary personnel. Equally important, Watson knew marketing, and the Company's record in that area had not been good for many years.

Watson, a native Hoosier born in Winona Lake in 1916, had a wonderful childhood. Winona Lake, the "home of Billy Sunday," was on the Chautauqua circuit. As a boy he attended Shakespeare plays all summer long, heard John Phillip Sousa, and saw Will Rogers. Watson's father was a man of little education, but he became a successful dry goods salesman. He made enough money by the time he was twenty-seven to sell out and pursue his real passion, saving souls. He attended the Moody Bible Institute and engaged in various charitable enterprises;

he was secretary of a leper's mission in India and business manager for a tuberculosis hospital in Kentucky. From time to time, he had to go back to work to make enough money to continue his charitable pursuits. In 1929 Watson's father went to work for the national Chamber of Commerce, selling the *Nation's Business* magazine. He came home for Christmas vacation in 1933 and received word not to come back. A victim of the Depression, Watson's father made one last sacrifice for his family, the sort of sacrifice with which American insurance companies were all too familiar in the 1930s. He committed suicide. He hoped that his modest insurance policy would see his family through the Depression.

Watson was raised thereafter by his mother and two older sisters. He was an enterprising youth. At eight years of age he began work selling magazines, and he worked at some job every year thereafter until his retirement. He graduated from Warsaw High School and went to Purdue University, the only college he knew anything about, to study architecture. Within one term, however, he realized that most architects were starving for work in the Depression, and he decided to transfer to Indiana University to take a pre-law course. This he combined with business courses and a lot of outside work to earn his way through college. Watson worked in a drycleaning business, in the campus book store, in his fraternity house, and in the library on a program provided as Depression relief for students. Watson graduated in 1939, having found it easy to get B's without much work.

Watson worked for several firms after graduation and became a pilot in World War II. Over Ploesti on July 15, 1944, Watson's B-24 was hit by flak. The co-pilot managed to get the plane back to its base 500 miles away. Watson's injury was serious and resulted in the amputation of fingers from his left hand.

Watson was self-conscious about his injury and somewhat depressed. When he told an acquaintance that he would like to get some job where he could use his education and sit in the far corner of an office, his acquaintance replied that the only place in the area where he could do it was The Lincoln National Life Insurance Company. Watson applied for work in the newly burgeoning Group Department and started work in 1945. A medical examiner told the person who hired Watson within Watson's hearing that the candidate's health was fine but that "all amputees have mental problems."

Watson quickly defied this analysis, overcame his reticence to meet the public, and took a job in the field, selling group insurance in Chicago. When he started at the Lincoln, there were only six people in the department, and he rose to the head of the department quickly. Menge and Rood were impressed with his abilities.

Watson never dreamed of the Presidency of the Company. Yet when the assignment came he did not feel unprepared for the task. After all, he had experience with a complete organization in the Group Department, employing its own actuaries and involved with agencies. He felt that he had gained the job to solve the Company's steadily growing agency problems, and he thought almost single-mindedly about sales.

Young Thomas A. Watson is at left.

Realizing his need for assistance on the technical side of the business, he soon made actuary Gathings Stewart President of Lincoln National Life.

Watson's thinking turned to new directions for the Company. Not all of the Company's acquisitions had been without headaches. Halsey, Stuart & Co., Inc., a bond brokerage firm acquired with Chicago Title and Trust, gave the executives the most problems in proportion to its worth to the Company. The basic problem was relatively simple: the company dealt in a product that had never been a Lincoln specialty. It was a very different kind of business, and its salaries were far higher than those in the Lincoln and the rest of its affiliates. Its high pay scales robbed Chicago Title and Trust of promising employees. It was clearly easier to sell the company than to spend valuable time on these somewhat trivial problems. The Lincoln divested itself of ownership in 1973.

The decision to sell the Dominion-Lincoln Assurance Company, Ltd., in the same year touched more fundamental assumptions about the nature of the Lincoln's business. Though the English market looked attractive, it proved terribly difficult for Yankees to handle. The decision to have prestigious Lords as directors worked at cross-purposes with the basic idea behind the British company. These gentlemen tended to look down their noses a bit at hawking insurance. The first manager, British-born but with Canadian insurance experience, did not work well with British agents. A British manager, though he sold a lot of equity-linked business, also ran an expensive operation and was difficult for the Fort Wayne executives to control. As Watson readily admits, the decision to sell the company, with about 90% of its business linked to the stock market, looked awfully good a year later when the stock market fell disastrously from its highs of the "go-go years."

Clearly, Watson was thinking of turning away from the search for new and even exotic markets. There was a lot more money to be made if the Company could increase its share of the domestic American market only a small percent, and that was the market, Watson thought, the Company knew best.

The decisions to get out of the Philippines and Paris, though rooted in that new assumption, each had particular reasons related to the particular organization. CORENA was a good solid company, but it was difficult to tell whether its operations benefited the Fort Wayne Company or the French managers the most. It did not prove productive of good reinsurance contacts for the home office's reinsurance operation. The Philippines presented a political problem. Two years before the island's president became a dictator, Watson heard that it was likely he would do so. Nationalization of the Philippine company or blackmail through the threat of nationalization seemed likely.

Pulling back from some of the ventures into "foreign" markets was the negative side of Watson's solution to the Company's sales problems. Lincoln National Sales Corporation represented the positive side. The idea was simple: Watson wanted to spend 200 million dollars on expanding the agencies, and he wanted to give the general agents new incentives to build large and strong agencies to sell life insurance. The existence of the holding company Rood and Menge had established, Lincoln National Corporation, provided a mechanism by means of which the Company could invest large sums in its sales agencies. Rood had worked on one of the principal problems of incentives: there was very little to induce a successful general agent to recruit new agents and incur heavy expenses and risks late in his life. Most of the agencies incorporated when LNSC was formed so that the Company could invest more capital in their operations and so that the agency head would gain the psychological advantage of incurring corporate rather than personal debt. To head LNSC, Watson chose Howard Steele, whom he described as a very "frank talker" and "not a backslapper." Ironically, Watson, the sales specialist, chose an administrator whose style might be thought to appeal more to an actuary. Thus Watson met the problem of lagging sales with a new style of organization and a new man who fit that style. The Company had taken a new direction toward production-mindedness.

Watson was quick to see other new directions in which the Company should go. Walter Menge was the first Lincoln President to begin sprinkling his speeches with promises of action "without respect to race, color, or creed." He and Rood had worked on the problem of employing black people. The Company worked at first through the Urban League. Later, Rood hired a capable black dean from Fort Wayne's Central High School, who had good contacts with Fort Wayne's black community, to help with recruiting. Social conscience had been a vital part of Watson's upbringing. In 1973 he established Lincoln Life Improved Housing, Inc., to rehabilitate abandoned dilapidated homes in the central city near the home office and provide adequate single-family dwellings for low- and moderate-income families. LLIH leases the improved homes to carefully selected families for five years, subject to

Chairman of the Board Watson took a highly visible role in committing the Company to equal opportunity for women.

mortgages secured from local banks at favorable rates. Their monthly rent includes the full cost of amortizing the mortgage, taxes, and maintenance. At the end of the five years, the lessees can acquire the deed to the home for one dollar plus the assumption of the remaining mortgage payments. The result is the family's acquisition of the property at about one-half the original cost. Tax incentives allow the Company to sell the properties at the low price without loss. Fifty-two of the fifty-seven homes acquired by LLIH now have families in them, and twenty-three families have purchased homes under the plan. Since the homes are concentrated in one area, the improvements have a ripple effect in the whole neighborhood, and other owners imitate the improvements. Watson proved sympathetic to the women's movement as well. He moved to make the Lincoln a leader in offering employment opportunities to women, choosing M. Lou Grawcock to head the Personnel Department and establishing an assistant to work especially on these matters, Nancy Peden.

Watson describes his political beliefs as "conservative" but steadily liberalized since his youth in a narrowly provincial Protestant small town in which "Catholic" and "Democrat" were bad words. He is an independent in politics, voting Republican most often, but he did vote for Adlai Stevenson for Governor of Illinois and for President of the United States (he did not think, in the latter case, that being a general was good training for the White House).

New Directions

Dr. McMurtry lectured in Korea on Lincoln in September of 1959. His interpreter stands at right. McMurtry got the distinct impression in some locations on his Asian tour that the interpreter embellished his remarks.

In 1971 Watson had to hire a new Director for the Company's Lincoln collection; McMurtry would retire in the spring of 1972. He had had a splendid career in the Lincoln Library and Museum. He strengthened the collection in every area but was especially skillful in adding museum items—ranging from a wonderfully preserved Lincoln shawl to a curious partially bald Lincoln bust. He changed the museum's bulletin to a four-page heavily-illustrated monthly with space enough for scholarly articles of substantial length. He oversaw an important move from the fourth to the first floor of the Company building and a great increase in exhibits for the public. He was a member of the National Lincoln Sesquicentennial Commission and in 1959 toured Southeast Asia to lecture on Lincoln for the State Department. McMurtry was in the right field at the right time. He was present at the opening of President Lincoln's papers at the Library of Congress in 1947. With the hundredth anniversary of the Lincoln-Douglas Debates (1958), the 150th anniversary of Lincoln's birth (1959), and the Civil War Centennial (1961-1965), McMurtry's life was a ceaseless round of dedications and new discoveries. Sometimes he marvelled quietly that he got paid to do exactly what he wanted to.

When Watson initiated the addition of a seven-floor building (joined to the rest of the home office complex by a second-floor bridge over Calhoun Street), he authorized a further expansion of the Lincoln Library and Museum. The museum was moved to the new building, and sixty new exhibits were installed, arranged chronologically to tell the story of Lincoln's life from his birth in a log cabin in Kentucky to his fabulous sixteen-day-long funeral. Watson also honored the museum's first Director by renaming the new facility the Louis A. Warren Lincoln Library and Museum. In 1978 the museum likewise honored its second Director by establishing the annual R. Gerald McMurtry Lecture. Each May the lecture brings to Fort Wayne an outstanding authority on Lincoln (like Pulitzer Prize-winning historian Don E. Fehrenbacher in 1979) to deliver a paper on Lincoln.

Since he had gone to work, in a sense, at eight years of age, Watson hoped to retire after fifty years at the age of fifty-eight. This, of course, was impossible because he assumed the presidency of the Company

161ST AGENTS TRAINING SCHOOL
JUNE 12-14, 1978

Note the sociological differences in the Agents Training School in the 1950s (page 96) and this one in the late 1970s.

when he was fifty-five. But he did move fairly rapidly to put together a new management team and to designate his own successor. Watson prided himself on his managerial abilities and read his beginning psychology text book from college every year. He insisted on managerial training for all of the Lincoln's management.

By 1975 Ian M. Rolland emerged as Watson's successor. Rolland was born in Fort Wayne in 1933, the son of Scottish immigrants. His father was an electrician who was able to give his family a comfortable middle-class environment. Rolland had a happy childhood, did well in his courses at Northside High School and played on the tennis team there (he notes modestly that it was much easier to get on the team before the recent boom in interest in tennis in America). He attended DePauw University because of its outstanding academic reputation. His interest in actuarial science began as an undergraduate, and he worked in the summertime at the Lincoln to get a taste of the kind of work to which such interest naturally leads. From the summer of 1952 on, then, Rolland has been connected with Lincoln National Life. At DePauw he majored in mathematics and economics, toyed briefly with the idea of teaching, but decided on a business career. To further this ambition, he entered the University of Michigan to study actuarial science. On his first exam, more difficult than anything he had ever seen at DePauw, he got a 28 and figured that his hopes of becoming an actuary were dashed. However, it turned out that this was the second highest grade in the class. He earned a Master's degree in one year and returned to Fort Wayne to work full time at the Lincoln in 1956.

Rolland was disappointed when his first assignment sent him to the Group Department, then located in a separate building on Wayne Street. This seemed at first like banishment from the "real" Lincoln Life, but he quickly became absorbed in the work and gained valuable experience in dealing with the sales force that many actuarial trainees did not get. Moreover, Thomas A. Watson was the head of the department, and the department was small enough to bring even this lowly employee into considerable contact with the man who would become the Company's

New Directions

Ian M. Rolland.

President in fifteen years. Watson marked him right away as a man of great promise.

Ambition for the presidency was the furthest thing from Rolland's mind. He has a talent for concentration on the task at hand, and that task was to complete his actuarial examinations. Study for these was a single-minded preoccupation with him, as Rolland's wife will readily attest. Rolland still had a longing for the Harrison Street office, and, when offered a choice of staying with the Group Department or moving to another job, he chose the other job, work on individual health insurance. Rolland moved afterwards to the Actuarial Department. He completed his exams in 1961 and at last (and somewhat impatiently) felt he was ready for a big assignment.

Actuary Sam Adams counselled patience, but the assignment came quickly. The week after he completed his last exam, Rood summoned him to his office and requested that he determine how much capital the Company should use to establish its new corporation in New York. Rolland spent all weekend on the problem (not exactly what his wife had in mind so soon after completion of the ordeal of the actuarial exams) and suggested a figure of five million dollars. Rolland then went to work handling the New York company's actuarial problems—indeed, most of its contacts—in the home office. It was extremely valuable experience, for Rolland had his first chance to deal with the problems of a *whole* company.

In truth, this New York venture had serious problems from the start. The Lincoln decided simply to build a little Lincoln Life in New York. But New York is a special market because of its tough insurance laws, a heritage of the old Armstrong investigations which indirectly brought Arthur Hall to the Lincoln. New York strictly regulates agents' commissions and the amount of money a company can spend on its agencies. As a result, the New York market is oriented toward brokers and independent agents, and companies must compete for their attention with price, product design, or service. The Lincoln wanted to use an agency system and ratebook like the ones it used in other states. Moreover, the Lincoln was a giant in the industry, and it could not help but to go into New York with a big-company outlook. The office was located in the heart of Manhattan's high-rent district. Watson later tried to salvage the New York Company, but it was doomed from the start and became in the end another of the operations he decided to abandon.

Rolland had no responsibility for the overall profitability of the New York Company, of course. He gained valuable administrative experience from working with it. Rood recognized Rolland's abilities, and in 1966 asked him to develop a new product line for the Company, variable annuities. Beginning with only a secretary, Rolland quickly built the variable annuities operation to about 150 people and was recognized throughout the industry as an expert on this new product. This experience added an element of independence to Rolland's thinking. There was no one within the Company who could give him guidance; he had to build this new department on his own.

Watson and Gathings Stewart (right) retired at the same time.

In 1970 Watson asked Rolland to help solve new problems in the Company's important Reinsurance Department, plagued with personnel problems. Rolland agreed somewhat reluctantly. At first, the job Watson offered seemed not to be any better than the one Rolland held in his rather independent variable annuity domain. But Rolland was a good Company man, he took the assignment, and he quickly learned that the reinsurance job was a very large one indeed. Three years later Watson, never afraid to make tough management decisions that do not court popularity, fired the head of the reinsurance operation and replaced him with Rolland.

As late as 1975, Rolland still had no inkling that he might ever head the Company; it was hardly even an ambition. Watson, who had no desire for (indeed, does not think it wise for a corporation to desire) a long presidency, had other ideas and gave Rolland important assign-

New Directions

ments that at last gave him the clue that he might be the next President. In 1977 Watson retired as Chairman of the Board and chief executive officer.

Rolland regards two policies as the most important in his tenure as President thus far. He became convinced immediately that Lincoln National Corporation needed more sophisticated and longer-range planning. A corporate planning group in the life insurance company and similar groups in all the affiliates now demand five-year plans of all the departments. Rolland thinks good managers should spend more time on planning even though they generally get more immediate gratification from "putting out fires." Second, he has created more cohesive Corporation-wide management. The top executives of all the affiliates now meet four times yearly, and Rolland hopes that, without destroying their autonomy, all will begin to feel themselves members of Lincoln National Corporation rather than bosses of independent fiefdoms.

Rolland stresses planning in part because he sees a more difficult and somewhat hostile environment for the Company in the future. Inflation and more intense competition seem certain parts of the future environment, and consumerism seems bound to bring a market that will demand more information about the Company's product before buying it. He expects the economy to grow more slowly than it has in the past, and he is certain that this factor demands increased productivity for the Corporation to maintain its record of success.

A key to Rolland's management style lies in his solution to the problem of productivity, a program in the Lincoln which is called "Quality Commitment." He describes it as a "humane" solution, and he particularly dislikes those corporations which hope to solve the problem, for example, by announcing flatly that they will fire ten percent of their management. He prefers to work more slowly for solider gains in the long run by enriching jobs to comprehend more complete parts of the Corporation's tasks and thereby eliminating jobs which can more appealingly be handled as parts of other jobs.

Words like "humane" come easily and convincingly from Rolland's speeches and memoranda. In the 1960s he was active in establishing the East Wayne Street Center, a community center which serves the needs of Fort Wayne's inner-city residents. Rolland was at first a member of the Evangelical United Brethren Church, and he took considerable interest in arguing for a liberal theology (he later became a Methodist and now attends the Unitarian Church). In whatever community he participates, he generally works for "outreach," and he readily admits that in the process of reaching out to those in need, his originally conservative political opinions became more liberal (a factor which was never held against him by the Lincoln's management). He voted for Robert Kennedy in Indiana's 1968 primary. He is proud of the increasingly active role the Company takes in the Fort Wayne community, a role symbolized by the Company's new sculpture garden, which for the first time brought the Fort Wayne public into contact with the works of America's greatest modern sculptors.

Indiana Governor Otis R. Bowen and President Rolland inspect George Sugarman's painted aluminum sculpture, Black Prow. *Sugarman, born in New York City in 1912, was educated at the College of the City of New York. One critic called his early polychromed wooden pieces "sprawling, baroque complexes of . . . brightly colored laminated wood, cantilevered and zigzagging into space."* Black Prow *is a simpler, more controlled work, which Sugarman created in his usual manner. He makes small cardboard models in his loft studio and paints them with colors from his dozens of small pots of paint. A fabricator constructs the large metal sculptures from the models.*

100

Richard Stankiewicz (above) created the large untitled piece in the Lincoln National Life sculpture garden pictured at left. Born in Philadelphia in 1922, Stankiewicz had his first one-man exhibition in New York City in 1953. Examples of his work are in the collections of the Museum of Modern Art, the Whitney Museum, the Solomon R. Guggenheim Museum, the Walker Art Center in Minneapolis, the Art Institute of Chicago, the Tel Aviv Museum in Israel, and the Joseph H. Hirshhorn Museum and Sculpture Garden in Washington, D.C. He typically forms welded steel into severely geometrical compositions.

Sculptor Bill Barrett (above and right, with Rolland) was born in Los Angeles. He attended high school in South Bend and is a graduate of the University of Michigan. The youngest sculptor represented in the Company's sculpture garden, Barrett works in brushed aluminum. LVII, shown here, is typical of the expressionism of Barrett's work.

George Sugarman talks with Mrs. S. Allan Jacobs, for several years the Company's advisor on art purchases. Mrs. Jacobs was responsible for acquiring the majority of the paintings and prints in the home office.

George Rickey's <u>Two Open Rectangles Excentric Var IV</u> is a popular sight in Fort Wayne. Passers-by often stop to watch the intricate movements of the wind-driven blades. Rickey, who was born in South Bend, spent his youth in Scotland. He received his B.A. and M.A. from Oxford. He returned to America in the 1930s. Beginning work as a mural painter, Rickey made his first mobile sculpture in 1945. His interest in such things doubtless came naturally to this son of a mechanical engineer and grandson of a clockmaker. His "useless machines" depend on motion rather than form for aesthetic effect. Rickey is widely acknowledged to be the leading spokesman of kinetic art.

New Directions

Rolland feels that being chief executive officer has moderated his political opinions. He knows that he has become more conservative fiscally. Despite his demand for planning, he sees the Company's position as essentially sound and ready for the future. The tremendous infusions of capital into LNSC have worked at last to boost the Company's agency sales force to levels of excellent growth, and he is ready, conservatively, to work at decreasing expenses and at putting the sales corporation on a self-sustaining basis.

With the addition of the new seven-story building and the acquisition of "Lincoln West," a large office building in suburban Fort Wayne vacated by Magnavox Corporation, the Lincoln's physical expansion is at an end for the foreseeable future. This is not to say that the management does not contemplate future growth of the business — far from it. But the management is committed to handling that growth with efficient use of its current work force. Increasing automation and computer technology must be used to make the present number of home office employees capable of performing the new work. Management frankly contemplates no increase at all in the number of workers in the home office for some time.

The long tradition of seeking acquisitions of good insurance companies for the Lincoln is very much alive. In 1979 the Company acquired the Security Connecticut Life Insurance Company of Avon, Connecticut. Security Connecticut does not maintain an agency force of its own. It sells entirely through independent insurance agents. Rolland feels that the addition of a company adept at brokerage business is an important diversification for the Lincoln. It gives greater marketing flexibility and puts the Company in a position of readiness for almost any future development in the realm of insurance marketing. Moreover, Security Connecticut is a fine company. In 1979 it wrote two billions of new business. When added to the 2.8 billions sold by Lincoln National Life in 1979 as well as the sales by American States and the Dominion, it makes the Lincoln the fifth largest writer of individual life insurance.

Rolland's management is a blend of tradition and innovation and brings to mind a factor which ties together all the reminiscences which made this brief history possible. Past and present workers alike, Lincoln National's employees reflected willingly and happily about the Company's history. The past of the Lincoln National Life, as the current advertising campaign stresses in regard to the Company's name, is definitely "easy to remember."

President Rolland.

APPENDIX:

These men were the initial founders of Lincoln Life:

		Subscription
Samuel M. Foster	Industrialist, banker	$5,000
William B. Paul	Life Insurance Agent	5,000
Daniel B. Ninde	Lawyer	5,000
Hubert Berghoff	Industrialist	5,000
Gary Brabrook		2,000
J. W. White	Banker	2,000
W. C. Rockhill	Industrialist	2,500
F. K. Safford	Food Wholesaler	3,000
H. N. McKee		5,000
Robert Millard	Food Wholesaler	2,000
J. McKay	Food Wholesaler	3,000
F. L. Smock	Food Wholesaler	2,000
G. A. Rabus	Tailor — Men's Store	3,000
E. W. Cook	Banker	2,000
C. H. English	Physician	2,500
W. J. Vesey	Lawyer	3,000
F. L. Jones	Proprietor of Laundry	2,500
Henry Beadell	Proprietor of Department Store	2,000
Fay P. Randall	Automobile Dealer, Realtor	2,500
Wallace E. Doud	Real Estate	3,000
Perry A. Randall	Lawyer, Industrialist	2,000
Arthur F. Hall	Life Insurance Agent	5,000
George W. Beers	Industrialist	1,000
M. J. Blitz	Insurance	1,000
Paul Mossman	Capitalist	1,000
Aaron Rothchild	Capitalist	1,500
R. B. Hanna	Lawyer	500
W. W. Shambaugh	Lawyer	500
C. F. Pfeiffer	Real Estate, Loans	500
John C. Heller	Title Abstracter	500
E. W. Dodez	Manufacturer Dental Supplies	2,000
Maurice I. Rosenthal	Physician	2,500
Ben Lehman	Men's Store	1,000
Jacob Funk	Treasurer Allen County	500
John N. Pfeiffer	Real Estate	500
Robert S. Taylor	Lawyer	500
B. D. Angell	Broker	500
Wm. Hahn	Merchant, Dry Goods	1,000
W. F. Moellering	Food Wholesaler	3,000

These subscriptions accounted for $87,000 of the original $100,000. Before the company opened for business in September, the following subscribers made up the difference:

	Subscription
Dr. S. H. Havice	$ 300
Dr. W. W. Shyrock	100
August Bruder	500
Charles Falk	500
Abe Levy	300
Gustave Berghoff	2,500
Dr. W. H. Johnson	1,000
M. A. Mason	100
E. H. Merritt	1,000
Theo. S. Seemeyer	500
C. J. Schieman	600
Simon J. Straus	2,000
Harry S. New	1,000
George T. Moore	500
Clinton Willson	100
W. K. Noble	5,000
W. H. Wiebke	600
J. A. Rossell	200
W. J. Probasco	1,500
F. M. Smith	100
S. H. Baker	500
J. F. Vordermark	100
Charles L. Henry	1,000
Otto Brown	1,000
Max B. Fisher	500
F. L. Stapler	500
George Ashley	200
Ben Lehman	1,000
C. E. Archer	500
Wm. M. Griffin	5,000

On the back fly leaf: The Lincoln's home office complex in 1980.